3—

1/5/24

# THE NORTHWEST

# AMERICAN DESIGN

# THE NORTHWEST

Text by Linda Humphrey and Fred Albert
Photographs by Michael Jensen
Foreword by J. Jackson Walter,
President, The National Trust for Historic Preservation
Introduction by Virginia and Lee McAlester
Design by B.W. Honeycutt

Produced by IMG Publishing

BANTAM BOOKS   NEW YORK   TORONTO   LONDON   SYDNEY   AUCKLAND

THE NORTHWEST

A Bantam Book / October 1989

Library of Congress Cataloging-in-Publication Data

Humphrey, Linda.
The Northwest / text by Linda Humphrey and Fred Albert;
photographs by Michael Jensen; foreword by J. Jackson Walter;
introduction by Virginia and Lee McAlester; produced by IMG
Publishing.
p. cm.—(American design)
Bibliography: p. 237
ISBN 0-553-05398-1
1. Architecture, Domestic—Northwestern States—Themes, motives.
2. Regionalism in architecture—Northwestern States. I. Albert,
Fred. II. Jensen, Michael. III. IMG Publishing. IV. Title.
V. Series.
NA7224.H86   1989
728.3′ 7 ′09795—dc19        89-442  CIP

*Published simultaneously in the United States and Canada*

Bantam Books are published by Bantam Books, a division of Bantam Doubleday
Dell Publishing Group, Inc. Its trademark, consisting of the words "Bantam
Books" and the portrayal of a rooster, is Registered in U.S. Patent and Trade-
mark Office and in other countries. Marca Registrada. Bantam Books, 666 Fifth
Avenue, New York, New York 10103.

Printed in the Italy by New InterLitho S.p.A.—Milan
0 9 8 7 6 5 4 3 2 1

To my children, Ben and Matt,
whose independence and good humor
make all things possible.

—LINDA HUMPHREY

---

To M. S., whose wisdom and spirit
inspire me always.

—FRED ALBERT

---

To Ann, whose support and sacrifice
made this possible, and
to Peter and Claire.

—MICHAEL JENSEN

# ACKNOWLEDGMENTS

In producing this book we wanted to give a sense of the Northwest as a place where people live in concert with the land—be it urban, island, country, or near desert. The Northwest is not all tall timber, rugged coastline, and sinuous waterways. Both eastern Oregon and Washington are arid climatically, and Idaho's terrain can be downright inhospitable. Yet snaking its way through the barren landscape of southern Idaho flows a river of immense proportion and power, offering life to desert moonscapes. One of the homeowners has taken refuge on the rugged cliffs surrounding this Snake River Canyon. Others have chosen bucolic settings: land on the San Juan Islands, forested city enclaves, or pastoral farmland. Still others have opted for the hum of urban life; they are modern pioneers who have assisted in the reclamation of decaying downtown areas. All are representative of the rugged individualism that has always characterized the West. We wish to thank them all for their cooperation, good humor, and inexhaustible hospitality: Leo Adams, Bob and Mary Alexander, Rob Anglin and Peggy Hackney, George and Pam Carlson, Lanny and Pat Carver, Rick and Bonnie Eiber, Wallace Huntington and Mirza Dickel, Jean Jongeward, Thom and Oy, Laz, Greg and Kathy Maxwell, Jim and Katherine Olson, Barbi Reed and Bill McDorman, Phil Sherburne, George and Kim Suyama, Henry Whiting and Lynette Kessler, and the few who wish to remain unnamed.

Finding these homeowners would not have been possible without the help of friends and professionals along the way. For steering us in the right direction we thank: Elizabeth Walton Potter, Helen Marshon, Nels Reese, Art Troutner, Dick Ritz, John Berg, Gordon Walker, Nelson Miller, Ernest Lombard, David Leavengood, Dick Wagner, Shirley Collins, Karen Jaenicke, Randall Schalk, and the Floating Homes Association. For lending their professional expertise we are grateful to Tom McCallum, whose encouragement and love of architectural history permeate this text, and to Larry Kreisman, Doug Kelbaugh, chairman of the Department of Architecture at the University of Washington, Peter Miller, H. L. Burt Holmes, Pietro Belluschi, Stuart Silk, Tom Bosworth, Arne Bystrom, James Cutler, Lasse K. Jaakola, Arthur Hart, Sol Zaik, William Fletcher, Greg Cleveland, Terry Hunziker, and Jim Ruscitto. For their personal assistance and hospitality we are indebted to Tiger and Geri Warren, Grace Kenyon, and Donna and Ken Fuller. And for finding us and supporting us as the project unfolded we thank Anita Davidson, Cam DeVore, Angela Miller and Sharon Squibb of IMG Publishing, and Coleen O'Shea and Becky Cabaza of Bantam Books. Grateful thanks also go to Larry Balin, Margie Beyer, Mae Reid-Bills of *American West* magazine, Gracelyn Blackmur, Jackie Burton, Jonathan Foote, AIA, Misty Haley, Bruce Hawtin, Vince Lee, Rick Pratt, Steve Shinek, Gerald Spence, Roger P. Strout, AIA, Iris Sutton, Ken Thuerbach, John Vaughan, and Daniel F. Williams, AIA, Price-Ragen Company, Naga Antiques Ltd., and the Seattle Public Library.

# CONTENTS

WASHINGTON

6

PIONEER FARMHOUSE                                    12
Simple Splendor on Decatur Island

TIMELESS ARCHITECTURE                                26
A Retreat on San Juan Island

MOUNTAINTOP MINIMALISM                               38
Squares, Cubes, and Spectacular Views
Overlooking Snoqualmie Valley

HILLSIDE HIDEAWAY                                    52
A Guest House with a Story Just North of
Seattle

URBAN SANCTUARY                                      62
Harmony of Art and Architecture in a Pioneer
Square Condominium

REGIONAL ORIGINAL                                    74
A Designer's Personal Perspective Atop
Queen Anne Hill

CITY BEACH HOUSE                                     88
East Meets West in an Architect's West
Seattle Home

FLOATING HOMES                                       100
Creative Living on Five Seattle Houseboats

INDIAN ANCESTRY                                      116
A Mosaic of Land and Life in Eastern
Washington

# OREGON

▲▲▲▲▲▲▲▲▲▲▲

**130**

# IDAHO

▲▲▲▲▲▲▲

**170**

STATE OF THE ART LOFT
**An Industrial Warehouse Takes on New Life in Downtown Portland**
**136**

HISTORIC HOMESTEAD
**A Pioneer Farm on Oregon's French Prairie**
**146**

COASTAL CLASSIC
**Rustic Simplicity on the Grassy Dunes of Gearhart**
**158**

LAKESIDE ARTISTRY
**Swedish Charm in an Idaho Cottage**
**176**

WRIGHT LEGACY
**Architectural Restoration Above the Snake River**
**190**

MOUNTAIN MAGIC
**Solar Technology in Sun Valley**
**200**

STUCCO AND TIMBER
**A Sun Valley Home Draws upon Southwest Archetypes**
**214**

FOREWORD **xiii** SOURCES **228**

INTRODUCTION **3** BIBLIOGRAPHY **237**

# FOREWORD

The people of the Northwest have a special relationship with their environment. One has only to look to this unique American region's architecture to prove the point. Whether the roots of their style are called International, Modern, Post-Modern, Oregon Rustic, or National Park, whether a simple cottage, a warehouse condominium, or a grand lodge, Northwesterners design with a keen appreciation for being part of their environment.

This approach to architecture is a key part of the Northwest's heritage. And, increasingly, Northwesterners are realizing that historic preservation offers the means of maintaining the strong and special connection between structure and scene, between man-made and natural environments.

Take one example. Oregon's seventy-four-year-old rubble-stone and cedar shingle Crater Lake Lodge is a rustic retreat exemplifying the turn-of-the-century cultural dynamism that linked protection of unique natural resources and scientific values with public recreation and scenic tourism. However, six years ago the National Park Service proposed tearing down the aging structure because it needed major restoration work and because it was perched on the rim of environmentally fragile Crater Lake. A major lobbying campaign—spearheaded by the Historic Preservation League of Oregon and the National Trust and supported by people all over the Northwest—demonstrated that restoration was environmentally safe and feasible, and led to a Park Service change of heart.

This lodge holds personal meaning for thousands of Northwesterners and other Americans. It has a long history in a relatively young state and it gives visitors a direct personal connection with history and with one of the scenic wonders of the world.

Crater Lake Lodge is an architectural statement and at the same time a harmonious part of a spectacular natural environment. It poses a challenge of stewardship that the people of the Northwest will surely meet.

The owners of the houses shown in *The Northwest* also understand that spirit of stewardship. For them, appreciation of heritage and environment become two facets of the same issue, an issue that Northwesterners care deeply about and invest considerable resources in—the quality of life and the continuity of American culture.

The owners of these houses, old and new, all share that basic commitment.

**J. JACKSON WALTER**
**President**
**National Trust for**
**Historic Preservation**

xiii

# THE NORTHWEST

# INTRODUCTION

The Northwestern states, isolated from population centers to the east and south by heroic mountains and endless plains, have become a unique outpost of architectural independence in our increasingly homogeneous nation. Blessed with an almost limitless supply of premium-quality timber, the Northwest is still dominated by houses sheathed in wood, even though most of the country switched to fashionable veneers of brick or stone during the early decades of this century. In style, as well as in materials, Northwestern houses illustrate a sort of middle-of-the-road conservatism in which traditional designs can seem almost modern in their simplicity, while modern designs seldom lack some reference to an older architectural heritage.

In the 1920s and 1930s informal building traditions of the region were developed into a formal movement that came to be known as Northwest Regional Architecture. The movement's principal spokesman was the Italian-born architect Pietro Belluschi, who arrived in Portland, Oregon, in 1925 and became an articulate proponent of house design for the next thirty years (one of his most memorable houses is delightfully highlighted in this book as "Coastal Classic"). In a lecture delivered in 1941 at the Portland Art Museum, Belluschi summarized the twelve essential elements of Northwest Regionalism:

First of all, there is the architect himself; second, the person for whom the house is to be built; and third, the relationship between client and architect. If there is no basis for understanding, the whole enterprise is an unhappy one.

Fourth. The surrounding country—the form, color, and general aspects of the landscape on which the house is to be placed. A house may suit the mood of the countryside, the color of the soil, the shape of the trees, and the texture of the grasses, or it may dominate them.

Fifth. The orientation—not only the location of the house, but that of the windows and their shapes will be affected by this consideration.

Sixth. The climate will affect the materials which give the house its appearance, and the roof, which more than anything else affects its form.

Seventh. Surrounding buildings and the existence of a strong stylistic tradition. Their presence cannot be entirely disregarded. The new house as far as it is practical should be made to harmonize with its neighboring buildings, however without abdication of ideals.

Eighth. The methods of construction, which vary from region to region, and which depend on the habits of the local craftsmen, on the practical setup of the building machinery, and on the custom of the people. If machine fabrication would really effect great economies, then it should be considered.

Ninth. The materials at hand.

Tenth. The financial restrictions of the client.

Eleventh. The physical requirements, based on the size of the client's family and on his standard of living and on his special hobbies.

Twelfth. All the mechanical equipment which has been created by this machine age and which is to be incorporated in the fabric of the house.

If we relate these different elements creatively in one unified whole, then we have modern architecture.

3

This concept of modern, therefore, will not lead us to expect it to be just another style. It cannot be labeled international style, although certain characteristics are universal, not modernistic. It should not even be called modern, because it goes back to fundamentals. It goes back to nature, if the owner's life is one of response to it. Therefore, we may deduce that a region with similar natural and human attributes may have an architecture harmonious to them. The people are neighbors, their interests are alike, they respond the same way to life, they have the same materials at hand, they have similar landscape, the same climate. So "regionalism" really has a meaning, which internationalism does not have.

Most of the sixteen charming houses surveyed in this book reflect in some way this unique Northwestern adaptation of Modern architecture. Many of the houses were designed by architects who have rejected what they consider to be the artificial and ever-changing fashions of architectural "style." Instead, they have looked to the lives and needs of the people who will use the houses in order to shape timeless dwellings "from the inside out," as advised by Belluschi. This book is therefore less about formal housing styles than about varying life-styles, and the unique and fascinating houses these have produced.

In an appropriate tribute to our country's seminal role in the early Modern movement, three of the houses are recent restorations of designs by two great masters of early Modernism and one of their followers. The earliest is "Regional Original," the house on Seattle's Queen Anne Hill designed by a colleague of Frank Lloyd Wright's. This house has strong overtones of Wright's distinctive Prairie Style, which was the pacesetter for domestic Modernism in the first two decades of this century.

Next comes a late design by the master himself. "Wright Legacy," built in 1952, was one of the last residences Wright designed and is his only work in Idaho. Crumbling through neglect a mere thirty-five years after construction, the house was rescued by a sensitive architect-owner who was able to retain most of the house's original furnishings and character. The lack of right angles in this house is typical of Wright's last works, including such well-known buildings as New York's Guggenheim Museum and the Dallas Theater Center. In the Idaho house he uses 60 and 120 degree angles almost exclusively.

Finally there is the previously mentioned "Coastal Classic," one of the masterpieces of Pietro Belluschi. It clearly demonstrates his principles, outlined above, in its clean and understated lines.

As these examples clearly attest, there has been an exciting rebirth of interest in preserving the work of early Modern architects, many of whom even designed the furniture to fit their houses. First popularized almost simultaneously by the Greene brothers in Pasadena, ca. 1905, and by Frank Lloyd Wright in Chicago, ca. 1900, furniture design soon became a passion with many architects. Few early houses still retain these furnishings—one imagines them disappearing in 1950s garage sales—and the owners represented here are to be saluted for treasuring the rare survivors.

4

Five other houses featured here are also in the Modern tradition, but have been built or totally redesigned in more recent decades. Each, however, still stresses some aspects of Belluschi's Regionalist credo.

In "Mountain Magic" the clients' conservation-minded life-style dictated the siting and technological needs of a unique solar house. This emphasis on energy self-sufficiency shaped the design, with traditional materials and craftsmanship playing a visible but clearly secondary role.

"City Beach House" is closest in feel to the Northwest Regional Architecture of the 1930s and 1940s. Designed as the architect's own house, the materials, roofline, and interior massing are all unusually responsive to the occupants' life-style.

A third example, "Timeless Architecture," also reflects many of Belluschi's principles and resembles an early folk house in its strict simplicity.

Some of these same principles are found in "Hillside Hideaway," but this time much of the structure is, surprisingly, concealed underground. In this unique guest house, respect for the site, invisibility from the main house, and ease of climate control take precedence in design.

"Mountaintop Minimalism," resembling two giant sugar cubes, is the most visually dramatic. Unlike most houses of the Northwest style which suit the mood of the surrounding countryside, this one takes a different approach to Belluschi's fourth cardinal rule and dominates it. Even here, however, the pristine white walls are made of traditional wood, in this case pressed-wood panels. In any other part of the country the walls would almost certainly have been constructed of stucco-covered masonry.

Still other, very personal, adaptations of Modernism are illustrated by "Indian Ancestry" and "Stucco and Timber."

Three other dwellings mirror the surprising diversity of inner-city living in the Northwest—on houseboats ("Floating Homes"), in a converted warehouse ("State of the Art Loft"), and in a dramatic high-rise apartment ("Urban Sanctuary").

Finally, the book includes three houses with more traditional roots. "Pioneer Farmhouse" and "Historic Homestead" are modern restorations of simple farm dwellings. The third, "Lakeside Artistry," is a new house charmingly designed to resemble a traditional Swedish farm cottage from the last century.

In summary, then, *The Northwest* treats a unique and intriguing collection of intensely personal dwellings. Almost all achieve the harmonious union with nature that is a cardinal principle of Northwest Regionalism. Furthermore, each reflects Belluschi's beloved closeness between designer and client, an interaction that, at best, creates not architecture for the masses but houses individually tailored to the life-styles of their occupants. Browsing through these sixteen houses emphasizes how successfully this is being achieved in this most individualistic corner of our vast country.

VIRGINIA AND LEE McALESTER,
Authors of
*A Field Guide to American Homes*

# WASHINGTON

Popular mythology would have you believe that Washingtonians are a web-footed lot who row to work in small boats through schools of leaping salmon. That view is not entirely inaccurate when applied to inhabitants of coastal Washington, that verdant strip of land bounded by the Pacific Ocean on the west and the Cascade Mountains on the east. Umbrellas are required, many westsiders do boat to work, and the Hiram Chittenden locks in Seattle have given many tourists a cameraful of leaping salmon. To promote the myth of swampy terrain and sunless skies, Seattleites proudly sport T-shirts and bumper stickers proclaiming "Seattle Rain Festival: Sept. 1—May 1." As members of "lesser Seattle," they discourage tourism and other sorts of "foreign invasion" in order to keep the area to themselves. However, their good-natured misanthropy has not deterred the rest of the world from discovering that the Pacific Northwest is not necessarily the rain capital of the world (New York has a higher average rainfall). The climate is remarkably temperate with mild winters and balmy summers and when the sun shines, Seattle, the "Emerald City" is a stunning jewel in the crown of the Pacific.

The real misconception is that the cloud-laden Washington coast represents the entire state. Quite the contrary. Drive over the Cascade Mountain Range to eastern Washington and the clouds will be hard to spot. This arid and often treeless stretch of terrain bears as much resemblance to its western counterpart as the Sudan does to Norway. Spokane, capital of the "Inland Empire," presides over one of the most productive and successfully irrigated agricultural areas in the nation. Even the Olympic Peninsula with up to 200 inches of rainfall a year and wilderness that no man has ever seen, bears little resemblance to the Puget Sound Basin, a bustling center of commerce and Pacific Rim trade. Washington is a state of intense contrast, more so than any other state in the nation.

The architects who followed Storey shared a reverence for materials and craftsmanship. However, they were significantly influenced by the modernist movement. Luminaries such as Paul Hayden Kirk, Paul Thiry, and Roland Terry in Seattle, and Pietro Belluschi and John Yeon in Portland drew upon the spatial concepts of the international style, the sequencing of interrelated spaces, and the use of standardized materials and clean lines, but with an interpretation all their own. The modernist imperative inspired their work, but regional romanticism softened it. They adapted the international style to the climate, the building materials, and the building practices of the Northwest. They built structures that were responsive to the environment, designs that integrated the setting and the landscape. These houses shared common characteristics: an open and simplified, yet functional plan, broad sheltering pitched roofs to protect from the rain and pine needles, long expanses of window to admit the light from different angles, the ubiquitous natural wood as a structural and design element, and a decided lack of decoration. Belluschi summed up this regionalist response by saying

that it went back to nature, as if the man and his environment were one. It was an architecture of place—an architecture that extolled, celebrated, and defined the uniqueness of the Northwest.

The advent of more sophisticated building technology, the scarceness of timber, and the influence of an ever more universal architectural vocabulary has diluted the purity of this 1930s—1960s tradition. But the natural impulses that inspired a Northwest Regional School still permeate the architecture and design of the Northwest. While architects draw upon the vocabulary of early forms as well as the cultural tradition of this rugged corner of the nation, they are not immune to flirtation with a more eclectic impulse. Seattle in particular has always been a magnet for gamblers and men of fortune. In contrast with the skyline of Portland, well modulated and goal oriented, Seattle's skyscrapers engage in a muscular jockeying for position, screaming for attention, eager to stand out. Residential architecture has struck a more contextual tone, but not necessarily a homogeneous one. Architects and designers are still striving to imprint the Northwest with their own unique and individual expressions of what constitutes "Northwest Style." Whether the underlying influence be Arts and Crafts, Modernist, or post-Modernist, an insistence upon informality and a respect for Washington's natural beauty characterize their work. Yet whatever testimonials may constitute the legacy of this architectural generation, we are all reminded by the 1981 eruption of Mount St. Helens that no matter how thoughtfully we impact our environment, ultimately Mother Nature will have the last word.

Seattle, unplanned and haphazardly settled, benefited from the lack of special interest groups dictating its future. Emerging as a roll-of-the-dice settlement of blue bloods, midwesterners, black-sheep Easterners, Scandinavians, Yugoslavs, Chinese, Japanese, its very diversity made it the most spirited and progressive community in the Northwest. Three men of vastly different character emerged as the founding fathers of Seattle: Arthur Denny, the civic leader, David S. (Doc) Maynard, developer and con man extraordinaire, and Henry Yesler, owner of the first steam-operated sawmill. This trio of ill-matched leaders pushed the city toward expansion and growth at the expense of any architectural consistency. A paucity of women contributed to a weak sense of community values, and by the time the disastrous fire of 1889 leveled the business district, there was almost a sigh of relief. Now the city could resurrect with purpose and planning.

The turn of the century marked the beginning of self-conscious Seattle architecture. The Olmsted Brothers, whose father designed New York's Central and Brooklyn's Prospect parks, among others, were hired to lay out a system of parks and boulevards, which in turn opened up a number of new residential areas. The first grand homes commissioned by pioneer industrialists were predictable clones of East Coast prototypes—grand and imposing, but hardly indigenous. The first indications of a style more suited to the Northwest appear in the craftsman-style houses of Ellsworth Storey. Storey, a graduate of the University of Illinois, arrived in Seattle in 1903 and set about to design houses on a modest scale. Thoroughly steeped in the Arts and Crafts style, and reserved by nature, Storey offered a simpler, more honest approach to Northwest design. By stripping away some of the elaborate ornamentation and superfluous detailing of previous styles, he adapted the craftsman style to the informal life-style that is the hallmark of Northwest living.

Long before white settlers set foot upon this land, native Indians had lived in harmony with the land, and save for a few wintering structures, had left it virtually unmarked. The white man's history begins with a somewhat nomadic fur-trading population whose presence marked the beginning of a long history of trade with the East. Captain Robert Gray established trade with China, exchanging furs for silk, tea, and spices, which he brought to the East Coast. Before more permanent settlers arrived, the Hudson Bay Company extended its influence throughout the Oregon Territory, that vast stretch of land that eventually was carved into the states of Oregon, Idaho, Washington, and Montana.

In contrast to the development of Oregon State, where men of solid Anglo-Saxon values sought the establishment of community, Washington lured adventurers in search of the wealth to be had in gold, timber, fishing, and furs. Cities sprang up for the sole purpose of outfitting this freewheeling clientele—fortune hunters bent on getting rich quick in the great Northwest.

One of the first Northwest cities to capture the markets created by prospecting was Port Townsend. This bustling harbor at the northern entry of Puget Sound filed a land claim in April of 1851, six months before settlers staked a claim to the tract now known as Seattle. Port Townsend was the first Northwest community of like-minded citizens intent on establishing roots. Public and private structures reflect a serious concern with permanence, mimicking nineteenth-century East Coast architectural styles. Fortunately, much of this legacy has been preserved. Visitors today can revel in a panoply of Renaissance and Romanesque Revivals, Greek and Classical Revivals, and all the Italianate detailing and Queen Anne embellishment characteristic of the High Victorian period.

Alas, Port Townsend's hopes of dominating commerce in the Northwest came to a crashing halt when the transcontinental railroad chose Tacoma for the Washington terminus. The railroad came to dictate the fortunes of many aspiring hubs of industry. Spokane was linked by railroad to the East, partially as a result of the vast lodes of silver, copper, lead, and zinc discovered there. In spite of being passed over for Tacoma, the entrepreneurial citizens of Seattle built their own line. Ultimately their efforts brought enough publicity to attract the Northern Pacific Railroad, and that link secured Seattle's ties to the rest of the country.

# Pioneer Farmhouse

## SIMPLE SPLENDOR

## ON

## DECATUR ISLAND

The view from the hillside above the farmhouse extends west to Lopez Island in the distance, and tiny Trump Island, uninhabited save for the deer that swim over, and one errant sheep whose successful navigation of Lopez Sound is still a mystery.

Ancient board and batten siding weathered to a cinnamon glow kept the owner from demolishing the house. Boots stand ready for a morning walk through dewy fields and muddy garden beds (LEFT).

The Pacific Ocean carves its way into Washington State at the northwest corner of America via the Straits of Juan de Fuca, which separate the Olympic Peninsula from Vancouver Island, British Columbia. Strung out like so many jewels upon a shimmering sea, the San Juan Islands stretch just north of the straits, protected by the rainshadow of the Olympic Mountains, and offering idyllic retreat for those pastoral souls desiring absolute tranquillity.

Officially numbered at 172 (at least 172 have been named), the tally of islands often tops 700 at low tide, then diminishes with the pull of the moon. All are parts of a vast and ancient mountain range, weathered and made habitable by the shifting tides. A solid granite core attests to their cataclysmic genesis, a base that restricts the amount of water available, thus forming a natural barrier to runaway construction.

The islands were discovered by a Greek navigator, Apostolos Valerianos, who was sent in 1592 by the viceroy of Mexico to explore the Northwest. Renamed Juan de Fuca by his Spanish benefactors, the pilot entered the Straits of Juan de Fuca and sailed for twenty days down the inlet, naming islands and believing himself to have found the fabled Northwest Passage. He returned to Europe as a self-proclaimed hero only to be followed by two centuries of misadventurers who missed the twenty-mile wide opening and came to believe that Valerianos's maps were mistaken. Finally, in 1788 British captain Charles William Barkley, using Valerianos's logs, found the passage, but the first successful exploration of the San Juan Archipelago occurred in 1792 when Captain George Vancouver took a surveying trip of the islands.

Today, four of the islands are served by the Washington ferry system: Lopez, Orcas, Shaw, and San Juan. The others are reached by private ferry, airplane, or private boat. Decatur Island lies just off the northeast tip of Lopez, and is one of the closest islands to the mainland. Inhabitants commute by private boat for the most part, although a grassy airstrip services a small commuter airline operating out of Anacortes (the mainland ferry terminus). Float planes taking off from Lake Union in the heart of downtown Seattle arrive in Decatur's sheltered bays after about thirty minutes of gliding over whale pods, virgin stands of timber, and eagle nests.

The beauty of the fieldstone chimney (TOP LEFT) induced the owner to save the house in spite of advice from well-meaning friends who urged him to raze the rotting hulk. The glacial conglomerate is composed of quartzite, slate, and aggregate, stones of tremendous variety and coloration.

Antique farm implements, a buck saw and a garden cultivator, (BOTTOM LEFT) once used by the original homesteader, recall simpler days.

**T**he original barn is built from cedar logs, individually charred to preserve against insects. The basic structure is a square with a hay loft in the middle and a large milking area. The side sheds housed the smaller animals.

**G**oats have the run of the 470 commonly held acres, just as the owners do.

**G**radually the owners have added some formality to the garden (LEFT). The height of the columnar plants, Irish junipers, balances the strength of the surrounding fence.

Phil Sherburne, owner of this turn-of-the-century farmhouse, came to Decatur at the urging of developer Jim Youngren, who needed guidance in developing a 485-acre parcel on the west side of the island. Sherburne, then director of physical planning for the city of Seattle, had been toying with a job change, but owning or developing vacation property had never been high on his list of priorities. "I had decided against recreational property in the past for all the reasons everyone cites: I didn't want to go to the same place all the time or maintain a second home." In spite of his reluctance, Sherburne took the short float-plane flight from Seattle, took a quick walk around the property, and the rest, as they say, is history. "In probably thirty minutes I had decided to leave my job with the city, do a recreational development, have a vacation home, and rebuild the farmhouse. All my rational reasoning went by the boards."

Sherburne offered to develop a plan for the property in exchange for the farmhouse and accompanying acreage, which had so captivated him. He felt that if he spent a number of months restoring the farmhouse, he would gain a sense of the island and thus be better able to preserve the

property's natural beauty. Youngren agreed, and soon made Sherburne his partner and gave him full management control of the development. For five months he worked on the house, toured the San Juan Islands, and ultimately arrived at a plan unique among recreational developments. Seventy-seven building sites were carefully chosen for their views, sun exposure, and privacy. Each site was a circle of ground no greater than one hundred feet in diameter. In total, these sites consumed only fifteen acres of property. The rest was to be held in common by the site purchasers, including the entire waterfront.

However, Sherburne's greatest challenge lay in the restoration of the farmhouse. In spite of its romantic appeal, the house had some very real problems. Uninhabited for nearly a decade, except for a motley group of sheep, the house appeared to be rotting at its foundation. When Sherburne called upon his friend and architect Tony Puma for advice, Puma took one look at the structure and told him to raze it. But Sherburne didn't want to lose the picturesque fieldstone chimney and the weathered color of the exterior siding. He had also grown enamored of the farmhouse's history.

It had been built around 1917 by one Roy Harmon, a Massachusetts-born man in his twenties who was on his way to Alaska. Stopping at Decatur to visit friends, he settled and never left. Reportedly, the plans for the farmhouse came from a *Popular Mechanics* magazine. Roy cleared the land, built all the split rail fences and the log barn, and ultimately married Sarah Matilda, a local girl. Sarah died after a few years and soon Roy found another woman named Sarah Matilda working at the local restaurant. Roy competed for her hand with another Decatur bachelor. He won, but Sarah announced to him that she wanted a washing machine and a refrigerator. Not even Roy's estimable talents as a fiddler at the local dances could persuade Sarah to ask for less, and so they struck a deal: a washer and a refrigerator in return for her agreement to keep him stocked with pie.

Roy and the second Sarah Matilda remained in the house until 1971 when Sarah's children by a former marriage, fearing for their parents' health, persuaded them to move to Anacortes, the nearest mainland city. As Sherburne sorted through the house debris, he found remnants from the Harmons' life together. Empty boxes of valentine candy, maga-

**T**he dramatic hillside garden (FAR LEFT) was originally laid out by the first homesteaders, Roy and Sarah Harmon. Now terraced with grassy areas, raised herb and vegetable beds, rose gardens, and a berry cage; the lower part is anchored by a newly constructed gazebo.

**T**he berry cage (MIDDLE LEFT) shields its harvest of raspberries, blueberries, marionberries, strawberries, grapes, and currants from the birds and raccoons by means of overhead wire netting.

**H**ydrangea beds provide color at the lower end of the garden (ABOVE). The lattice and cedar log sections are lagged together with bolts that permit easy disassembly should the owner need to move heavy equipment into the garden.

**19**

zines, and a couple of Sarah's dresses provided personal glimpses, while receipts for the selling of wool attested to the very real business of running a farm. Roy raised sheep and sold raccoon skins. It turned out that at the same time Roy was selling raccoon skins to Sears Roebuck, a very young Phil Sherburne, raised on a dairy farm in Rainier, Oregon, was trapping and selling muskrat skins to the same company.

Digging through the flotsam of other people's lives gave Sherburne respite from the tedium of rebuilding rotting walls and decaying foundations. Three sides of the house required new structural walls (the exterior is largely facade), and the new foundation had to be poured using the "bucket and crawl" method. As the house was jacked toward a vertical position for each new bucket of cement, the house began to make audible resistance. The creaks and groans made each vertical increment a test of endurance. How much creaking could the house take before snapping the coveted chimney, and how much groaning could Sherburne take before he threw in the trowel. "We got it pretty close," Sherburne admits. "Then we just had to stop."

The interior walls on the first floor were eliminated to give the house a one-room feel. Sherburne loves to step out of bed and walk right to the kitchen, a place where he feels most comfortable. The stairway and upper bedrooms are all washed with sun from the skylights he installed. And a first-floor bedroom gave way to a bathroom—a luxury the Harmons never knew.

The upstairs had been used primarily for storage. However, Sherburne saw this as a prime guest-room area and began to tackle the heavy paper sheeting on the walls and ceiling. He pulled back the water-soaked ceiling fiberboard and quickly discovered a bee's nest "probably two feet in diameter." Poking around gingerly, he expected the house to be swarming with bees at any second, but instead found the mass teeming with millions of carpenter ants. His confrontation with Mother Nature did not end here. A few weeks later, while prying up the ridge cap on the decaying shingled roof, he was startled by a series of bats that emerged one by one from their protective cover. "We had it all," Sherburne muses, "carpenter ants, bats, sheep, and raccoons."

**T**he steep staircase (LEFT) is relatively the same as its original prototype; any replacement with more gradual treads would rob living space. The major change was to capture closet space by enclosing the stairwell.

**A**n inveterate table sitter, the owner enjoys ruminating at mealtime under the twelve dollar kitchen window found in a salvage yard (ABOVE RIGHT). From this window the sheep can be watched coming down the hill, lambs bouncing at their sides, and the skittish evening deer.

**M**ission chairs discovered at a Seattle garage sale flank the frisée upholstered thrift shop sofa. An old ice chest serves as side table, while a Northwest Indian painting hanging over the fireplace recalls the original settlers of these islands (RIGHT).

**G**enerous skylights flood the upstairs bedrooms with sunlight and convert what was once a dusty storage area into comfortable and private guest quarters (BELOW).

**T**he first floor bedroom (RIGHT), incorporated into the general living area, is only a few steps away from the kitchen.

Sherburne still battles the raccoons in the unprotected orchard. However, the soft-fruit portion of his large garden is entirely protected from predators. The Harmons had a country garden on the sloping water side of the house. When Sherburne saw some old pictures of their garden, he was determined to plant it in similar fashion, but the plantings could not be protected from the deer. Thus the decision to build an enclosure fence. The width was established by the existing garden. However, the length became a product of what Sherburne thought was an ingenious Thai solution to keeping deer at bay. He had read about a low wall with screens and horizontal sticks that animals were presumably

wary of negotiating. Not wanting to compromise the view with a fortresslike fence, he opted for the stick-and-screen method at the lowest point of the slope, only to discover that the deer were a lot smarter than he thought.

The present fence is constructed of island materials: fieldstone and cedar logs. Lattice panels are lag-bolted to the logs to permit easy disassembly, should Sherburne need to move a tractor or other heavy materials into the garden. A berry cage on the south side is trellised above to protect the soft fruit and grapes from birds and the wily raccoons. The cage houses red and black currants, gooseberries, strawberries, raspberries, marionberries, grapes, and kiwis.

The garden is divided into four distinct sections: the upper section or raised beds are for vegetables and herbs; the rock beds down the sides are for flowers and shrubs; and the berry cage is separated by wire netting. At the very foot of the garden a gazebo and pond form a quiet retreat quite separate from the other sections. The paths in the upper garden are defined by the raised beds and copious lavender, which defines the path opposite the rock beds. The continuity of lavender is evident throughout the garden, an herb attractive not only for its flowers and smell, but for its shape and robustness. Sherburne has experimented with a number of unusual vegetables, the most successful being a group of artichokes at the bottom of the rock beds. The harvest has been more than ample, and the gray-green foliage provides beautiful contrast. Gradually, Sherburne has added some formality. The four columnar plants, Irish junipers, give some height to the garden to balance the strength of the fences.

Aesthetics aside, the whole reason for having the garden was for eating and cooking. Sherburne and girlfriend Michele Cook spend their weekends preparing meals from the garden. "I get an extraordinary amount of pleasure out of going out first thing in the morning and picking fresh raspberries for my cereal," Sherburne says. "It makes all the work worthwhile." Michele derives special pleasure from the dried flowers she stores and weaves into wreaths and arrangements. She has been particularly influential in the recent design of the garden, adding a number of plantings suitable for dried bouquets and potpourri.

Like his predecessor, Roy Harmon, Sherburne loves pies. The thirty to forty fruit trees Harmon planted in the orchard provide ample bounty for this passion, and give Sherburne and Cook surplus for sharing with friends and neighbors. The sense of community is nowhere more evident than on winter evenings when friends gather to cook and listen to National Public Radio. "Our life here is the antithesis of the cocktail party," Sherburne muses. "We thrive on rituals and definition, and small gatherings of friends." Sherburne feels that he has gotten to know Roy Harmon over time—in the split rail fence, the hard work, the big leaf maples, and the locust trees he planted. "I enjoy the continuum, the contrasts of life," he adds. "It's such a change from the city."

The big drafty fireplace from the original house was replaced with this efficient wood stove (ABOVE).

Propane fired gas range (FAR TOP LEFT) is bordered by rich green tiles, a more pleasing countertop solution than the more economical plastic laminate they first installed. The kitchen is open to the entire house and invites participation from family and friends.

Canning jars filled with dried herbs and flowers line cabinet tops (FAR MIDDLE LEFT). Zinnias, lavender, strawflowers, rose petals, lemon verbena, chamomile, lemon balm, and lemon marigold are used for potpourri and wreath-making.

Herbs are picked from the garden when flowering, then dried for seasoning, decoration, and fragrance (FAR BOTTOM LEFT).

# Timeless Architecture

## A

## RETREAT ON

## SAN JUAN ISLAND

**F**rom a distance, the bent profile of the roofline resembles wings settling into the landscape. Architect Tom Bosworth designed the porch knowing that it would be a major part of the house in terms of time spent. He contained the porch by creating a solid railing, thus giving a sense of enclosure on inclement days. The steps are purposely grand—much bigger than needed on a functional level—for sitting, reading, and relaxing. The informal wooden love seat (LEFT) provides a comfortable spot for viewing the scenery.

**T**he broad steps and generous porch invite casual use. Blustery days find the owners enjoying meals protected by the solid storm windows, while balmier weather makes a solitary rocker inviting moorage for whale watchers.

**T**he rocky promontory hosts a nineteenth-century obelisk (RIGHT), one of three such monuments used to locate the watery boundary between the United States and Canada.

Spectacularly situated on a San Juan Island rock outcropping, this secluded retreat seems as anchored to the site as the stands of virgin timber that blanket the surrounding topography. Here, the owners, a Seattle banker and an art historian, indulge not only their need for privacy but their connection with a simpler life-style and an abiding love of the land.

San Juan Island is the county seat of Island County, the only county in Washington State that cannot be directly reached by car. As such, it has the only incorporated town in the San Juan Islands, Friday Harbor, and an almost comic history of boundary battling and ownership disputes. First settled by the peaceful Salish Indians some 5000 years ago, San Juan Island is unique in Indian history for sheltering one of only a few tribes who practiced reef netting of salmon. The Salish occupied a rich and temperate land where food nearly fell into their laps and disease was relatively unknown. They were, however, subject to periodic invasions from the war-like tribes of the north and actually welcomed the arrival of white settlers in the early 1800s who brought stability and protection from the invaders. Unfortunately, the Salish were too susceptible to European diseases and by 1880 their numbers had been dramatically reduced. It was only through intermarrying and the introduction of western medicines that they finally rebuilt their population.

Meanwhile, British and American settlers of the San Juan Islands were trying to decimate each other in farcical rounds of bravado and confrontation. In 1846 representatives of the United States and the British Empire divvied up the North-west roughly at the forty-ninth parallel. Actually, the land was of little consequence to either the United States or Great Britain, who had much larger fish to fry (Britain had colonies worldwide, and the U.S. was battling over land in Mexico), so the wording of the treaty, which designated the U.S.–Canada boundary, takes the Oscar for vagueness. In a grandiose but poorly thought-out gesture, the United States conceded Vancouver Island and the Canadian Gulf Islands to Britain. The boundary line ran easterly along the forty-ninth parallel, but fell short of specificity as it traveled south through the straits separating Vancouver Island and the U.S. mainland. There are three channels separating the land

A quiet corner (TOP RIGHT) for escaping the fierce winds makes outdoor dining possible in any weather. Hot summer days find the storm windows raised, attached by heavy chains to the porch ceiling.

Patterned after the nineteenth-century farmhouse so typical of the San Juan Islands, the house (RIGHT) is meant to look as if it had always been there. Weathered cedar siding and a sheltering roofline give a sense of historical continuity and are at the same time highly practical.

A meandering road winds through the contours of the land, providing staccato glimpses of the house (FAR RIGHT), before the drama of its siting is finally revealed.

30

masses, and each country recognized a different channel of demarcation. American settlers invaded the islands with little regard for the British claim, and by 1859 angry words, fist-raising, and periodic military threats by the British brought the long-standing dispute to its rather comic breaking point. One Lyman Cutler, an American settler, shot a British pig invading his potato patch, and before too long 2000 British troops faced off against a motley crew of 460 Americans aching to resolve the rivalry once and for all. The fortuitous arrival of British Rear Admiral Robert L. Byers short-circuited any plans for real bloodshed when he announced that he would "not involve two great nations in a war over a squabble about a pig." The denouement of the great "Pig War" extended over a twelve-year period of joint occupation, with mutual attempts on the part of both British and Americans to impress each other with sumptuous feasting and revelry, until 1870 when Kaiser Wilhelm I of Germany, who was selected as an impersonal third party, arbitrated the dispute by awarding the islands to the U.S.

The 1980s have brought a different kind of confrontation to these island gems: big development versus gentle living on the land. Fears about runaway construction on these islands have made both full-time and part-time residents acutely aware of the necessity for thoughtful development of this national treasure. An intense respect for the land brought the owners of this 130-acre parcel of forest and rock to a meeting of the minds with Seattle architect Tom Bosworth, honored for his environmentally responsive designs. They wanted a weekend house, a minimum shelter, a solitary place for ruminative hikes, the gathering of family, and quiet pleasures such as reading—something unostentatious, something that looked like it had been there forever.

The result of their collaboration is a light-flooded, cedar-sided, handsomely porched great room with bedrooms at each end. The plan was simple and quite explicit: a large space in which to sit, rest, prepare food, and dine; two discrete bedroom and bath wings; and loft areas where their three grown children and friends could retreat. The design went very quickly once the site was selected, but Bosworth says, "They were having a real struggle over where the house should go. Actually they had taken extreme positions." There were open meadows, enclosed meadows, for-

**L**oft spaces at either end of the great room give overflow guests extra sleeping room. The three-foot-deep walls separating the great room and downstairs bedrooms provide ample room for sleeping niches, bookcases, and the slope of the ship's ladder.

**T**he kitchen (RIGHT) is entirely open to the living space. Open shelving makes dish storage convenient and easy for guests. The owners decided against a dishwasher to keep life simple. They counted on having enough free time to enjoy washing dishes.

**T**he loft ladder (BELOW) is modeled after companionways found in ships. Handholds are cut in each of the broad hardwood steps to give the climber a solid grip.

**T**he large pine dining table flips to make a pool table (RIGHT), a welcome wintery weather diversion.

ests of fir, cedar, and madrona, copses of trees, and the magnificent moss-covered barren rock that spills into the sea. The owners had been pitching a tent around the land for nearly a year. "We spent a lot of time tromping over the property," recalls Bosworth. The immense variety made the decision agonizing because there were twenty to thirty simply outstanding building sites. Inevitably they returned to the raw coastline. "I think there are several million building sites in the world with woods and water views," says Bosworth, "but there are very few sites where you can have exposed waterfront without any other structures around. It's almost a unique site."

Bosworth called upon the San Juan farmhouse vernacular (distinguishable by large wooden windows, stained exteriors, covered porches, steep-pitched gable roofs), but drew primary inspiration from the generously proportioned nineteenth-century summer houses on the East Coast. "I like to do work that is not identified to a particular era, a timeless look," says the architect. "I wanted to design a house that after you'd seen it, you would have trouble imagining the landscape without it." The result is a spare and weathered cedar exterior with interiors that seem to capture light from every angle. A pervasive design thread in Bosworth's work is the thoughtful positioning of windows and doors to allow for natural light. Handsome seven-foot French doors invite direct light from the water while transom windows above admit a more reflected light, muted by the porch overhang. Clerestory windows provide bright sunlight overhead while preserving the comforting sense of a sheltering roofline.

The silvery gray vertical exterior siding was to be balanced by horizontal bands of eggshell white on the interior walls. "White takes light sympathetically," explains Bosworth, "and is an old-fashioned detail." The contractor chose four-inch clear native cedar, intersticed, for the interiors, and when the installation was complete, the warmth of the yellow wood persuaded the owners to keep it natural. The painted bedroom walls have a pristine Shaker quality, but the golden tones of the great room are only enhanced by the day-long light moving across the mellow cedar surface.

The kitchen counter, which runs the length of the back wall, is purposely held back from the oversized windows in order to give visual elbow room. Open shelving allows easy

The master bedroom walls are painted eggshell white to reflect the morning light bouncing off the water. The bedrooms are positioned at either end of the great room to afford greater privacy.

Preserving a turn-of-the century farmhouse feel was a guiding principle in the design of the bathrooms (LEFT). Tubs, sinks, towel rods, and brass fixtures were found at salvage outlets. The Villeroy and Boch tiled floor, though new, is reminiscent of earlier tilework patterns.

Scrubby rocks at the rear of house are framed by a back porch window opening (RIGHT), designed to enhance the flow of air through the back door and to give greater visual connection with the outdoors.

access to tableware and display room for baskets, bowls, pots, and pans. A refrigerator, the hulking linebacker of most kitchens, is neatly hidden in an adjacent mudroom along with other less attractive kitchen accoutrements. A large pine table serves as catchall for myriad activities. At one time a jigsaw puzzle might be laid out at one end, graduate school applications pondered over at the other, and breakfast spread in between. Flip the tabletop and a pool table appears. "A bonus," say the owners, who spent months searching antique stores and salvage yards for the time-worn look of well-loved pieces.

The property faces south and west, and on most days the lofty spine of the Olympic Mountain range looms on the horizon. On very clear days, the southern tip of Vancouver Island, some ten miles away, is visible, and as night falls, the lights of Victoria echo the starry sky. An ancient obelisk on the property is one of three such monuments that are used to define the boundary separating the U.S. and Canada.

The fierce winds that sweep across this point made solid construction a must. Heavy storm windows blanket the porch, and a solid railing gives protection from the elements. "When the winds really let loose," the owners say, "it's almost like being in a ship at sea. The waves splash against the cliffs and sea spray hits the house." The house has proved to be airtight: no whistling wind or moaning air currents disturb their tranquillity. The storm windows are designed to be raised in warmer weather and secured by chains to the porch ceiling. On these days of zephyr breezes the family spreads out on the porch to watch the drama of sealife before them.

Killer whales swim by, breaching the water with their massive bodies. Locals who have studied the whales can identify

pods and individual whales within the group. The owners have adopted one of these whales as part of the fund-raising program started by the Friday Harbor Whale Museum. Eagles nesting in a nearby tree are so tame that they actually perched atop the obelisk as construction progressed, monitoring the activity. In the evenings they will often swoop down to raid seagull nests below the rocks and are then pushed back by the enraged gulls in a cacophony of squawking and screaming. Schools of salmon still ply these waters but the days of attaching a net between two canoes and scooping up the bounty belong to the early Salish. This family is learning how to use a rod and reel.

A quieter drama unfolds in the fields and forests behind the house. In the morning the ground is alive with hopping rabbits, and the forests secret deer and other shy creatures. The first thing the family does when they arrive is take a march around the property, checking fenceposts, wildlife, and vegetation. ''All the kids joke about the 'death march,''' they say, laughing. ''[Dad] goes at full speed around the perimeter, through brambles, holes, and puddles. No one can keep up with him.'' Then they relax, sprawling upon the broad porch steps or exploring the landscape.

In the first year the family played Johnny Appleseed, scattering California poppies and 500 daffodil bulbs across the property. The discovery of early homestead remains was made all the more poignant by the daffodils growing by the vestiges of a front door. They also found pottery shards in the dirt floor of their predecessors' home: ironstone that matched exactly their own pattern. These shards were lovingly carried home, a link with history, and another project in the endless array of possibilities awaiting folk who have found their link with the land.

# Mountaintop Minimalism

## SQUARES, CUBES,

## AND SPECTACULAR VIEWS

## OVERLOOKING

## SNOQUALMIE VALLEY

**T**he home's pristine sense of order and symmetry is in marked contrast to the rugged beauty of the Cascade Mountains.

**T**he home is remarkable for its consistent purity. To avoid hanging fixtures off the side of the house, uplights were recessed into the front stoop (LEFT). Even the landscaping is minimal, consisting of slender Italian cypresses punctuated by plantings of laurel.

**S**tand anywhere in Rick and Bonnie Eiber's hilltop home and the world spreads out before you like an emerald quilt. Here, twenty-five miles from Seattle, patchwork parcels of farm and forest drape the undulating terrain of the Snoqualmie Valley, while in the distance, the snow-capped peaks of the Cascade Mountains stretch for miles beneath a cloud-laden sky. Even for a region where breathtaking views are as plentiful as Puget Sound salmon, the sight is something to behold.

The Eibers' house more than holds its own against this awesome beauty. For instead of trying to blend in with their bucolic surroundings, the owners have chosen to confront them with a home whose intricate sense of order and precision is an invigorating counterpoint to Mother Nature's untamed splendor.

Dubbed "the sugar cubes on the hill" by pundits in the valley 1,200 feet below, the house is composed of two flat-roofed boxes painted a pristine white. While one box sits parallel to the hillside, the other rests at a seven-degree angle to its mate, adding a dash of unexpected tension to the ordered design and affording a slightly different view from each structure.

Each two-story cube measures approximately 1,000 square feet, with one designated for entertaining and the other for the family's private living quarters. The cubes are joined in front, but not along the back, creating a recess that the owners have transformed into a landscaped atrium. On days when the skies open up and fog shrouds the valley below in a blanket of white, the atrium is the center of attention. Rainwater collects in the center of the butterfly roof and cascades into two interconnected pools below. In a downpour the waterfall can be quite dramatic, especially when viewed from the window seat overlooking the atrium. "Everybody complains about the rain in Seattle," says Rick Eiber, a graphic designer. "We decided to turn it into an amenity."

The cubes are sheathed in MDO, a wood product normally used to make traffic signs. MDO is plywood covered with a resin-impregnated paper that resists the elements and retains a smooth finish when painted. In order to cover the seams between the sheets of MDO, architect Stuart Silk en-

The landscaped atrium provides a foreground focus for days when the view is fogged-in. During a rainstorm, water cascades off the rooftop scupper into the interconnected pools below.

cased the home in a grid of aluminum strips painted white. The strips form squares two feet by two feet—a module repeated in the window mullions and throughout the interior. Besides keeping the rain out, the grid lends a sense of scale and visual variety to the exterior.

Such understated adornment is unusual for Silk. Since moving to Seattle in the late seventies, the Yale School of Architecture graduate has made a name for himself as one of the brashest and most innovative voices in his field. His residential designs—blocklike forms marked by grand staircases, sculptural interiors, and classically inspired ornament—have garnered him widespread attention, as has his oft-quoted assertion that "wood is good for two things: painting and burning."

"There's no question I have an impetuous streak," says the architect. "I want to do things that are mischievous and daring. I'm too bored otherwise."

Silk is quick to admit that the Eiber house is a departure from his recent work, but not from his design philosophy.

"My goal is not to slam an idea down a client's throat, but to try and find something that's compatible for both client and architect—something that reflects what they want within my own boundaries of what I find interesting. And frankly, doing something like this is an interesting challenge because it's so minimal and so rational."

The Eiber house celebrates order and integrity by reducing everything to its purest form. All unnecessary elements have been eliminated or hidden. Cabinets are devoid of knobs. The TV is hidden in a wall cupboard and the china is stored on a cart that resides in its own garage off the dining room. The front entry is illuminated by uplights recessed into the front stoop so fixtures would not need to hang off the side of the house. Even the electric meter has been relocated to a position several feet from the home, hidden from view by a five-foot-high boulder, so as not to mar the purity of the exterior.

This purity continues in the interior, which the owners have decorated in an ascetic palette of white, black, and gray. The spareness of the color provides a gallerylike backdrop for both the scenery and the Eibers' collection of art. The latter is divided between primitive crafts and contemporary works by Northwest artists.

The exterior is clad in MDO, a wood product covered with resin-impregnated paper that is commonly used for traffic signs. The aluminum grid is both practical and ornamental, keeping water out of the MDO joints while lending a sense of scale and visual variety to the structure.

Decorative iron railings flank the second floor landing. The modified Versailles pattern repeats the house's gridded theme. Ceiling-hugging clerestories frame views of the adjoining hillside while capturing the last of the afternoon sun.

The stairs leading up from the slate-covered entry (LEFT) are treated with a black Swedish finish. The light trough at left highlights the owners' collection of primitive masks.

**S**mall, square windows circle the top of the double-height living room, which the owners have furnished with contemporary classics by Marcel Breuer, Le Corbusier, Mies van der Rohe and Eileen Gray. The grouping overlooks Snoqualmie Valley and the Cascade Mountains.

**W**.T. Wiley's drawing, *Looks like NUDErections in ART,* hangs to the left of a Massimo Vignelli sofa in the living room (RIGHT). The lacquerlike floor was made from Swedish-finished fiberboard inlaid with squares of black marble.

Rick Eiber sees a natural kinship between primitive art and his minimalist house. Both are attempts to express complex notions in the simplest way possible. "Eskimo drawings have all the basic elements of line, color, and form, and they're applied without cultural distortion so they become very pure," he says. In shaping their home, the owners have tried to distill a basic shape—a cube—into its purest and most concentrated form. Like the art within, its beauty is derived from its ability to convey a lot with a limited vocabulary.

The house is entered through a canopied doorway that leads into an entry hall surfaced in black slate. Straight ahead is the atrium, with its gnarled hemlock, pools of water, and view of tiny Fall City below. (Locals generally attribute the name to nearby Snoqualmie Falls, a natural wonder that's more than eighty feet higher than Niagara.)

To the right is the dining room and adjoining two-story living room, which the owners have furnished with contemporary classics by Marcel Breuer, Mies van der Rohe, Le Corbusier, and Massimo Vignelli. Small, square windows circle the top of the room, framing vignettes of the surrounding grass and mountains. At twilight, the windows wash the living room walls in gold and pink streaks of light.

The Eibers were interested in using the house as a testing ground for new materials. One of the more innovative applications is found in the living room, where two-by-two sheets of medium density fiberboard (a dense grade of particleboard) were laid on the diagonal and sprayed with a white water-based Swedish finish topped with a clear sealer. The resulting floor, which has been framed and inlaid with squares of black marble, closely resembles lacquer, but resists scuffing. Though beautiful, the results were achieved only after much trial and error. "We started out trying to create a dramatic floor at an inexpensive price," says the owner. "We ended up with a dramatic floor at a dramatic price!"

Crossing back through the front hall, one enters the kitchen with its forty-inch counters and central cooking island topped with pearly gray, white, and black granite. The adjoining family room features a breakfast table and a modular sectional that doubles as extra sleeping space for their daughter's slumber parties. Bonnie Eiber has an adjacent office where she can watch both the atrium and the view while doing the bookkeeping for her husband's business.

**P**atti Warashina's sculpture, *Mrs. Peabody,* rests on a console table painted by James Mason. Leather chairs surround a Le Corbusier table in the dining room (ABOVE), which features a photo by Gyorgy Kepes, calligraphy by Gesei Komai, and a Seattle Repertory Theatre poster illustrated by Fay Jones.

**T**he kitchen (RIGHT) features extra-high granite counters and an island fitted with a self-venting cooktop. Appliance garages at either end of the counter keep clutter out of sight.

The staircase to the second floor has been treated with a black protective finish. A light trough along one side highlights the owners' collection of masks by Eskimos and Northwest Coast Indians, as well as examples from Guatemala, Switzerland, Ecuador, and New Guinea.

The second floor landing overlooks the entry hall and serves as a bridge between the two cubes. To the right is Rick Eiber's den, which features built-in display space for the couple's collection of antique and contemporary pots from the Southwest. A column of glass blocks topping the front door is echoed in their daughter's bathroom, where the blocks have been sandblasted to let in light but ensure visual privacy. Sandblasted glass also appears in overhead light fixtures and as a shower enclosure in the master bathroom.

On a clear day, the Eibers claim they can see all the way to Canada, 100 miles away. They're also privy to constantly changing weather fronts, which can deliver hail, rain, snow, and sun within a single twenty-four-hour period. While the weather is often harsher on the hilltop, the owners are compensated by magnificent rainbows and the welcome surprise of driving home and finding sunshine on the summit when the world is socked-in below.

Having lived on the twenty-ninth floor of a Chicago highrise, the Eibers were determined to find a view lot with "foreground"—trees and vegetation near to the house that would lend a sense of scale to the scenery and frame the view beyond. The hillside in front of the house is lined with alders, while a smattering of firs and pines ensure that the view remains at least partially green year-round. Formerly timberland, the five-acre lot features an old logging road, which Bonnie Eiber plans to turn into a garden, as well as a forested ravine that is home to deer, coyotes, and bears.

The hillside across from the front door was hydroseeded with gold and russet grass interspersed with clusters of pampas grass. Columnar cypress trees line the front of the house at precise intervals, breaking up the austere facade. Lava rocks circle the foundation, providing a transition between the house and the surrounding plantings, which have been chosen to soften the severity of the structure without compromising its design. Future plans call for the addition of a third cube to house a garage, graphic design studio, and an extension of the family room. The cube will be canted at a thirty degree angle from the rest of the house, and will be connected to it by a twenty-nine-foot glass wall.

**T**he den overlooks the living room, the atrium, and Snoqualmie Valley. The thin black line along the baseboard helps to float the floor away from the walls.

**O**n the bathroom (FAR LEFT), a panel of sandblasted glass is an elegant alternative to a shower curtain, and allows diffused light to illuminate the commode. The photographs are by Marsha Burns.

**I**n the den, pieces of Northwest art glass top display shelves filled with Mexican and Native American pots (MIDDLE LEFT).

# Hillside Hideaway

### A GUEST HOUSE

### WITH A STORY

### JUST NORTH OF SEATTLE

YOU ONLY CAN UNDERSTAND SOMEONE OF YOUR OWN SEX
YOU OWE THE WORLD NOT THE OTHER WAY AROUND

The eroded edges of the concrete wall (decorously smashed by the architect himself) suggest an old ruin upon which the wooden house has been built. Along this entrance, the wall continues inside as a reminder of the hill just beyond.

The path from the main house meanders through the woods and ends at the top of the stairs (LEFT). The architect Jim Cutler designed the approach so that visitors would get their first look at the house when standing in the central courtyard.

Any visitor who has endured the punishing contours of a sleep sofa or the buzz saw snoring of a well-meaning host would appreciate the hospitality shown by the owners of this Seattle-area guest house. With its private driveway, full kitchen, laundry, terrace, and acres of closet space, this retreat gives new meaning to the expression "home away from home."

Architect Jim Cutler went to great lengths to preserve the privacy of both the owners and their guests. Taking advantage of the site's rolling terrain, Cutler buried the one-story, L-shaped house into the side of a hill facing away from the main house, rendering the guest quarters nearly invisible. A meandering path from the main house deposits visitors at the top of the hill behind the guest house. From there, a staircase steps down between the two wings of the house, ending up in the private courtyard below.

The 1,800-square-foot house is surrounded by towering firs and lush vegetation, creating the feeling of a hidden retreat in the woods. That sense is reinforced inside, where radiant expanses of ocher fir stretch overhead like the welcome boughs of a sheltering tree. Cutler has used fir everywhere—on the floors, ceilings, walls, cabinets, and window frames. By exposing the supporting trusses and posts, he's laid the structure bare, allowing the integrity of his materials to echo the purity of the setting.

Cutler's love affair with wood has been celebrated in more than 100 buildings since he set up practice in suburban Bainbridge Island in the mid-1970s. The architect's use of natural materials and sensitivity to light and locale recall the Northwest Contemporary Movement of the 1940s and 1950s. But he's infused this tradition with a look all his own, creating sculptural designs that are at once highly original and warmly evocative.

The guest house steps outside that pattern just a bit, blending into its natural setting and looking inward onto itself with an almost Oriental sense of introspection. The approach was partly programmatic, partly a response to the architect's own desire to design a house that not only pleased the eye but told a story, as well.

Recent personal experiences had left Cutler fascinated by the cycle of life, by issues of time and decay. He wanted to

The house's structure is laid bare through a visible system of posts and beams that continues inside the house. The concrete fireplace enclosure juts out at an angle from the surrounding wood walls, emphasizing the contrast between the two materials (LEFT).

All rooms open onto the private courtyard (TOP RIGHT), which architect Jim Cutler treated like an extension of the interior. Note the way the pavers dissipate into the surrounding landscape.

Artist Jenny Holzer created the white marble bench (RIGHT), which is inscribed with a variety of unusual aphorisms.

**T**he guest house also functions as a gallery space for the owners' art collection. Here, a lead painting by Jannis Kounellis hangs in the hallway adjacent to the living room. The concrete wall was sandblasted and tinted with a subtle hint of green for added interest.

**T**he wood framework of the house barely touches the concrete wall, adding to the sense of separation between the two elements. The translucent fiberglass ceiling admits a soft, diffuse light that brings out the color of the fir and accentuates the contours of the concrete (LEFT).

The kitchen (ABOVE) is open to the adjacent living spaces for maximum informality.

The fir interior radiates warmth. Interior designer Terry Hunziker kept the furnishings spare, emphasizing rounded shapes that soften the house's angularity. The painting over the fireplace in the living room (TOP RIGHT) is by Helen Frankenthaler.

The cooking island and cabinets are covered in clear fir (BOTTOM RIGHT). A Mark Di Suvero sculpture rests atop Terry Hunziker's slot-based dining table.

Corrugated cardboard chairs (FAR RIGHT) by California architect Frank Gehry combine art and function, and are surprisingly comfortable. Terry Hunziker designed the table, which is made from pickled steel fitted with half-spheres of black-stained oak.

see if he could express these complex notions through his architecture by choosing materials with different life spans and counterpointing them in such a way that they commented on each other: old vs. new, timeless vs. transient.

Cutler started by setting the building's wood frame within a fractured concrete shell, much the way one would pitch a tent on a platform at a campground. Rising out from behind the house and extending beyond its base, the concrete stands like the relic of another time—its jagged edges and sandblasted surface wearing the deterioration of time.

By contrast, the wooden house seems like a transitory intruder—all fresh and new but without the concrete's immunity against damage and decay. Subtle separations, like the wood boardwalks that float a quarter inch above their con-

crete bases, or the narrow air register that divides wood floor from concrete wall, heighten the dichotomy between masonry and lumber.

Cutler accentuated this division between materials by rotating the wood part of the house eight and one-half degrees from the axis dictated by the concrete shell. As a result, lines scored in the concrete floor aren't parallel to the surrounding surfaces. The concrete fireplace enclosure sticks out like a disjointed nose from the beveled cedar exterior. And hallways run from wide to narrow like some surreal sideshow attraction. But the visual tricks also serve a purpose. By shrinking the width of the front hall as it advances toward the bedroom wing, Cutler has created a psychological barrier that says "Do not enter" without the need for doors or signs.

Cutler left the concrete wall exposed along the back of the house, anchoring the interior while providing a physical reminder of the hillside beyond. The wall's craggy surface—shaded with a hint of green—is illuminated from above by a translucent fiberglass ceiling. Durable enough to walk on, the ceiling casts a diffused light that changes throughout the day, reflecting the fir's ruddy glow in the late morning and accentuating the concrete's texture at twilight.

Both the master bedroom and the children's bedroom open out onto the illuminated hallway. Cutler took advantage of the situation by surrounding the door to each chamber with sheets of sandblasted glass, which admit light but preserve privacy. Another interesting twist was placing a pair of pedestal sinks in a niche off the hallway outside the bath-

room, so that guests could wash up without intruding on those using the facilities inside.

At the owners' request, interior designer Terry Hunziker kept the furnishings spare, choosing rounded sculptural pieces that contrast with the house's angularity. The living room is dominated by corrugated cardboard furniture designed by California architect Frank Gehry. Patterson Sims, chief curator of the Seattle Art Museum and a friend of the owners, suggested the furniture after spying one of Gehry's Colorcore fish in the main house. Despite their packing-carton appearance, the chairs are surprisingly comfortable.

Hunziker designed the round, slot-based dining table and twin side tables, all of which are made from oak and pickled steel, repeating the house's juxtaposition of natural and man-made elements.

Aware of the owners' keen interest in art, Cutler left plenty of room for display. A lead painting by Jannis Kounellis dominates the front hall, while a Helen Frankenthaler rests atop the fireplace. The courtyard contains a white marble bench by Jenny Holzer inscribed with a variety of aphorisms, ranging from the droll ("Slipping into madness is good for the sake of comparison") to the sardonic ("Killing is unavoidable but is nothing to be proud of").

All of the rooms open onto the courtyard, which Cutler treated as a private extension of the interior. In one corner he erected an eroded concrete wall that helps define the space while suggesting some long-fallen structure. The area in front of the wall was to sink down into a muddy pond (a suggestion of further decay), but the owners were concerned about mosquitoes, so a planting of irises stands in its place. Thomas L. Berger Associates, the landscape architects, bordered the terrace with salal, twinflower, *Gaulnettya*, heaths, and heathers, while areas alongside the front entry feature clusters of deer ferns, sword ferns, and bunch-berry—woodland plantings that provide a natural transition between the house and surrounding forest.

With such tranquillity and creature comforts to recommend it, there seems to be very little trouble attracting guests. The only problem is, once they get there, who would ever want to leave?

**A** shower and toilet are situated in compartments on either side of the lavatory in the master bedroom (FAR TOP LEFT).

**P**edestal sinks were placed in a niche outside the bathroom (FAR BOTTOM LEFT) to capitalize on their sculptural quality and maximize the use of space.

**T**he master bedroom (TOP LEFT) features a bathroom en suite. Sliding doors permit easy access to the courtyard.

**T**he children's bedroom (BOTTOM LEFT) features built-in bunk beds with ladders that double as bookshelves. Sheets of sandblasted glass surrounding the doorway admit light but preserve privacy.

61

# Urban Sanctuary

## HARMONY OF ART

## AND ARCHITECTURE

## IN A PIONEER

## SQUARE CONDOMINIUM

**O**n the east wall of the living room, Jeffrey Bishop's indigo homage to fire is paired with Nancy Mee's glass-and-copper sculpture. Furnishings were kept light and flexible; a quartet of stools flank a centuries-old Italian armchair and its contemporary counterpart. Beveled edges and a recessed center make the ceiling seem to float overhead.

**T**he owners make their home atop the nine-story Olympic Block building (LEFT) in the heart of Seattle's historic Pioneer Square. Jim Olson collaborated with a team of architects and developers on the mixed-use structure, which respects its 1890s setting but is firmly fixed in the present.

**H**istoric Pioneer Square is a vibrant link to Seattle's nineteenth-century roots. Located at the south end of the city's central business district, the area is home to a rich treasury of late-Victorian and early-twentieth-century architecture. The district's offices, antique shops, galleries, restaurants, and theaters attract crowds both day and night, while the converted industrial buildings house some of the city's most colorful living spaces.

Originally the heart of downtown, Pioneer Square was built on the fortunes of the lumber mills, the maritime trade, the railroad, and the Yukon gold rush. Logs harvested along the forested slopes of what is now downtown were skidded down Mill Street for processing and shipment at the water's edge (giving rise to the term "Skid Road"). Hotel and retail operations sprang up around the shore in order to service the growing population.

Then, in 1889, a great fire ravaged Seattle, destroying twenty-five square blocks—virtually the entire city. The sensational story of the fire, and the reconstruction in its wake, attracted thousands of new residents, as well as a fair share of architects and builders. What started out as a tragedy ended up being a boom for the nascent metropolis.

The city wasted no time rebuilding its core. New ordinances dictating masonry or stone buildings led to the construction of solid three- to five-story structures in the Romanesque commercial style popularized by the famous East Coast architect H. H. Richardson.

In the years prior to World War I, businesses began relocating uptown, and Pioneer Square became a haven for warehouses and low-income, transient workers. New earthquake and fire codes following the Second World War proved to be the death knell for many of the buildings, which were destroyed or abandoned. Skid Road, the lumber district, became Skid Road, the vagabond district.

Initial attempts to restore parts of Pioneer Square following the 1962 World's Fair were greeted with enthusiasm, and in 1971 the area became the city's first historic district. Since that time, the neighborhood has been the site of numerous restorations and adaptive reuse projects, resulting in a strong mix of commercial and residential development.

The view from the kitchen terrace (FAR LEFT) encompasses nearly 100 years of downtown development, from the Richardsonian Romanesque Pioneer Building of 1889 (bottom) to the monolithic Columbia Seafirst Center of 1985 (far right).

The terrace affords a stellar view of the 1914 Smith Tower (LEFT). The forty-two-story structure was built by millionaire Lyman Cornelius Smith, of firearms (Smith and Wesson) and typewriter (Smith Corona) fame, and was for many years the tallest building west of the Mississippi.

▲▲▲▲▲▲▲▲▲▲▲▲▲▲▲▲▲▲▲▲▲▲▲▲▲▲▲▲▲▲▲▲▲▲▲▲▲▲▲▲▲▲▲▲▲▲▲▲▲▲

**A**rtist Ann Gardner created the kitchen backsplash from molten glass embedded with crimson curlicues of burnished copper. The piece is mounted on a mirror for added brilliance, and is illuminated at night by concealed lights. The cabinets are made from medium-density fiberboard that has been sponged and treated with clear sealant.

Architect Jim Olson has long played a key role in the revitalization of downtown Seattle. As a principal of Olson/Walker Architects from 1971 to 1985 and Olson/Sundberg Architects since then, he has had a hand in some of the city's most imaginative and distinctive buildings. Their eloquent concrete Pike and Virginia Building, snazzy Hillclimb Court, and exuberant, polychrome South Arcade Building frame three sides of the historic Pike Place Market district, proving that new architecture can be respectful of an old setting without being derivative or dull.

Having conquered the Pike Place Market, the architects turned their attention south to Pioneer Square, where the nine-story Olympic Block building now stands at the crossroads of one of Seattle's most famous intersections. Once the site of a venerable hotel, the lot stood empty for over a

decade after the building's collapse in the early seventies. The new structure, which Olson played a key role in both designing and developing, respectfully echoes the cornice, oversized windows, and Romanesque entry of adjacent buildings, yet asserts itself as a work of today. "We wanted to do a building that was more of a statement about our time and less of a statement about 1889," says the architect.

Jim Olson and his wife Katherine moved into the top floors of the mixed-use building back in 1987. While the windows at either end of the long, narrow townhouse afford spectacular views of the city, Elliott Bay, and the Kingdome, the real view is inside. Jim envisioned the residence as a sanctuary from the city, designing it like a cocoon with warm, enveloping spaces that prompt you to look inward, in both the physical *and* the spiritual sense.

**A**rt, antiques, and a warming fire make the kitchen a place to relax and read as well as prepare food. A colonial gateleg table from 1740 is paired with sleek leather armchairs. Barbara Noah's painting *Body Language and Signs of Communication* hangs alongside Rik Adams's iconographic fireplace surround.

Despite its scant 1,400 square feet, the home feels remarkably light and spacious. Inspired by sources as diverse as contemporary art and Egyptian tombs, the owner/architect sought ways in which to break through the interior's sheetrock boundaries by layering the ceiling and walls in each room and then cutting through the layers to reveal the spaces beyond. In some areas, the ceiling was suspended in the center of the room and the edge beveled to a fine point, so that the ceiling appears to be a thin plane floating beneath the actual ceiling (which has been painted dark to make it recede). In other areas, the ceiling is punctured by a succession of setbacks topped either by a skylight or an illuminated trough.

Even the living room floor seems to float in space, stopping about eight inches short of the surrounding walls and wrapping up the inside of a freestanding ledge that skirts the room. Although the floor most closely resembles granite, its rosy, cloudlike finish is softer and warmer, echoing the ruddy masonry cityscape outside.

The floor was made from squares of medium-density fiberboard that were cut and fitted into place, then numbered and removed for painting. Each piece was treated with two shades of oil-based paint applied with a sponge, then finished with a clear sealer. After drying, the pieces—over a thousand in all—were brought back to the condominium and laid into place like a giant jigsaw puzzle.

When the Olsons entertain, it's usually either an intimate get-together or a standing-room-only soiree. To accommodate such flexible requirements, the couple has kept the interiors spare, eschewing formal seating groups for more

**B**y layering ceilings and cutting through walls to reveal spaces beyond, architect/owner Jim Olson created the illusion of greater space within the 1,400-square-foot apartment.

**T**hroughout the house, familiar objects are interpreted in new ways. Here, entry columns (LEFT) are rendered in fused glass by artist Nancy Mee.

**L**ight refracted in a prism above casts a rainbow reflection across the "cosmic shaft" (RIGHT). The twenty-five-foot-high light well provides the condominium with a contemplative, inward-focused refuge from the hustle and bustle of the city outside.

casual compositions that counterpoint old and new. In the living room, a contemporary Italian easy chair covered in supple burgundy leather goes one-on-one with a centuries-old Italian armchair. A quartet of stools (picked up for a song in New York) and a leather-top desk with slender metal legs provide contemporary reinterpretations of traditional forms.

Seattle artist Jeffrey Bishop was asked by the owner to create a pair of twenty-foot murals for the living room walls. Working with the concept of "endless space and endless time," Bishop painted a pair of mystic vistas incorporating Giacometti-like figures floating against stellar fields of moody midnight blue. The eastern mural represents fire, while the opposite wall, toward Elliott Bay, depicts water.

Sculptor Nancy Mee collaborated with Bishop, creating freestanding columns of fused glass that complement each mural. Strands of glass stand like a frozen waterfall before the "water" painting, while stacks of triangular glass are sandwiched between collars of scorched copper in front of the other wall. Mee also created a narrow piece that is inset between the two windows on the living room wall.

"I love art in galleries and I understand why people buy it that way, but this, to me, is much more meaningful," says Jim Olson. "When you're sitting here, you're sitting *in* art."

The fusion of art and architecture was important to the architect, but he was careful to allow his collaborators free reign to create as they saw fit. "I wanted them to take risks and push their own art form as far as they could, because that's what I was trying to do with myself."

The art provides a focus for the interior, as does the twenty-five-foot-high light well piercing the center of the residence. Dubbed the "cosmic shaft" by the owners, the square, pale gray atrium is topped by a skylight fitted with a manually controlled oculus that opens and closes like the lens of a camera to control the flow of light. Daylight pouring into the shaft passes a set of four prisms that cast rainbow-colored refracted light against the walls of the light well. Clerestory windows lining the top edge of the shaft are ringed with shallow troughs of water that cast shimmering waves of light against the ceiling.

Artist Walter White, who devised the installation, first approached Jim Olson with the idea of shining rainbows on the side of an office building the architect was designing.

Although the owners of the building demurred, Olson contacted White when he began work on his own home.

When viewed from the adjacent hallway, the walls of the shaft recede—an effect the owner likens to the "whiteout" skiers encounter on a snow-covered slope. The Olsons find solace in their daily journeys through the lightshaft. Like meditation, the experience provides a momentary escape from outside stimuli. "You look into this thing and you can't tell where the walls of it are, so you imagine infinity," says Olson. "Trying to make space seem bigger and create feelings of infinity in a small space is very important. I would love to do an environment in space, where people are confined to a small area but you want to make them feel psychologically free. That's what a lot of this is about."

During football season, Katherine Olson can be found in front of the TV set in the downstairs den. This cozy alcove, right off the living room, is outfitted with a sleep sofa, bookshelves, and a collage that artist Robert Allen Jensen "remodeled" at the owners' request. In expanding his original piece, Jensen added the words "Complexity and Contradiction" along the bottom—a tongue-in-cheek homage to architect Robert Venturi, for whom Olson's firm acts as associate architect on the new downtown Seattle Art Museum. As for the rest of the piece's significance, Olson shrugs and says, "I think it's a lot about sex."

The stairs to the second floor wrap around the light well, leading to a closet-lined hallway above. Although the hall appears to dead-end at a blank wall, narrow passages flanking the wall lead to the Lilliputian master bedroom. Just large enough for a queen-sized bed, the room is expanded visually by the stepped ceiling and glass doors leading to the adjoining terrace. A miniature trundle bed accommodates the couple's dog, City Bear.

The kitchen is furnished with a diverse assortment of antiques, contemporary pieces, and art, creating an environment as conducive to reading as it is to cooking. A recessed skylight illuminates the mid-eighteenth-century gateleg dining table, which sits atop an old Afghani rug. Rik Adams, a designer in Olson's office, created the fireplace surround: a metal armature topped by flamelike ribbons of copper. Countertops are red granite tile (an affordable alternative to sheet granite), while the cabinets are fiberboard sponged to match

**M**ementoes from the owners' travels are kept in a bowl in the living room (LEFT).

**T**he house is a series of layered spaces and internal vistas, as seen in this view from the upstairs hall (ABOVE TOP), across the "cosmic shaft" to the living room below.

**J**effrey Bishop's two-part mural dominates the living room (ABOVE BOTTOM). The west side represents water, and is fronted by a frozen waterfall of fused glass by artist Nancy Mee. Floors throughout are crafted from painted fiberboard finished with a clear sealer.

71

the floors. Sliding glass doors open onto a flower-filled deck overlooking Elliott Bay and the Seattle skyline.

The highlight of the kitchen must surely be the backsplash created by artist Ann Gardner. Crimson curlicues of burnished copper bask in bubbly swirls of clear glass, which have been mounted against a mirrored wall for maximum brilliance. At night, low-voltage fixtures hidden behind the cabinets make the work positively glow with liquid light.

In the kitchen, as elsewhere, decorative objects have been clustered in vignettes to preserve the home's uncluttered ambience. A glass bowl in the living room is a repository for curios collected on the couple's travels—everything from dolls and shells to miniature urns and sarcophagi. A display niche off the stairway exhibits a cross section of icons, from Reis Niemi's bullet-punctured silhouette of a man saluting, to Greek and pre-Columbian figures, to a glass bone wrapped in a fabric splinter by artist Michael Aschenbrenner.

Opposing niches off the upstairs hall contain more treasures: an English bamboo wardrobe topped with a contemporary Northwest Coast Indian mask, and a dignified Chippendale highboy paired with a riotous reinterpretation by artist Pedro Friedeberg.

The owners have lived downtown since 1979, when the couple moved into Jim Olson's much-praised Pike and Vir-

**A**t 14,410 feet Mount Rainier is the tallest precipice in the Northwest and a dominant feature in the Seattle landscape. The mountain hovers over Beacon Hill in this view from the owners' bedroom terrace.

**T**he master bedroom (LEFT) boasts a view of the Kingdome, Seattle's domed sports stadium. The terrace plantings were designed by Becca Hanson. The necklace wall sculpture is by Sheila Klein.

ginia Building overlooking the Pike Place Market. At that time few people of means chose to live in the center of the city, which has long been plagued by transients and panhandlers. Today, high-rise condominiums dot the Denny Regrade area north of the commercial core, and the pioneer mystique has all but faded away (even if the transients haven't).

For the Olsons, living downtown means having a world of restaurants outside their front door and leaving for the theater at 7:55 and still making an eight o'clock curtain. Traveling to work is also easier. Jim Olson's architecture firm is just downstairs, as is Katherine Olson's office, where she manages the building's commercial properties.

"We could live our whole lives and never leave the building," the owner says, laughing. "If I want to work at home for a couple of hours to concentrate, I can come up here. I can take a nap or have lunch in the middle of the day and run back to the office. Instead of getting into a car I go running along the waterfront every morning. That's my commute."

The couple quells their cabin fever by escaping to their vacation cabin on the weekends. But come Sunday night, it's back to the city. "I always feel happy when I walk in the front door," says Katherine Olson. "I always think it's beautiful and it's special. I thought that about all our houses. I've never opened a door without really getting excited."

# Regional Original

A DESIGNER'S

PERSONAL PERSPECTIVE

ATOP

QUEEN ANNE HILL

The Seattle skyline serves as the backdrop for a living room still life.

Sunlight fills the breakfast room adjacent to the library (LEFT). An eighteenth-century Sheraton settee sits beneath a portion of a tapestry door surround, which once hung in William Randolph Hearst's San Simeon. Other portions of the tapestry were used to make the pillows below.

Just as colonial settlers looked to Europe for guidance in designing and furnishing their new homes, so Washington's earliest residents borrowed from the East Coast when shaping their new state. With no history to call their own, residents of this new frontier relied on traditional building styles and interior design practices to give their homes an instant sense of permanence.

With time, as a regional identity grew, Northwesterners began to turn their backs on the tastemakers 3,000 miles away, preferring to look locally for their design inspiration. What developed was a regional style tailored to the temperate climate and cool, gray light of Northwest skies. Natural and unpretentious, the look that became known as the Northwest Style glorifies the unadorned beauty of native materials and the spare, graceful lines of the Orient. Neutral colors carry the muted hues of cloud-dappled skies into the interior, linking the two in a harmonious whole.

No one has refined and glorified this look better than Jean Jongeward. For over thirty-five years, Seattle's doyenne of decorating has set the standard for Northwest interiors by combining an architect's understanding of space and function with an unerring eye for color, surface, and detail.

Jongeward holds fast to the principles she established early in her career: balancing neutral hues and natural fabrics with innovative applications of metal and plastic combined with one-of-a-kind works by artists and craftspeople. Through the years her interiors have been called everything from conservative to radical. But labels don't seem to bother Jongeward—her work speaks for itself. In commissions ranging from homes, offices, and restaurants to the governor's mansion in Olympia, Jongeward has demonstrated that good design is about more than knowing the rules, it's about knowing when to break them, as well.

The designer lives atop Queen Anne Hill, a residential neighborhood located to the north of Seattle's central business district. While the hill was originally named for the towered villas that dotted its slopes, few of these homes remain today. Gone, too, is the cable car that once ascended the hill's twenty-degree incline, abetted by a weighted truck traversing a subterranean tunnel. Progress, however, has not

The 1925 house is fronted by a paved terrace (TOP LEFT). Architect Andrew Willatsen, a former employee of Frank Lloyd Wright, evoked the master's Prairie Style through the use of a flat, broad facade covered with horizontal siding, which he topped with a stucco band inset with roof-hugging windows.

Eighteenth-century French garden furniture adorns the front terrace, which is lined with shrubbery for added privacy (BOTTOM LEFT).

The house commands a breathtaking view (ABOVE) of Elliott Bay and the Seattle skyline, dominated by the Space Needle at center. Early Seattle homes often ignored the vistas outside. In fact, when the owner tried to build her deck in 1960, none of the houses in the neighborhood had one, and even her architect tried to talk her out of it.

dimmed Queen Anne's appeal, which includes outstanding views, an attractive array of older homes, and some of the city's prettiest parks.

Jongeward's 1925 house was designed by Andrew Willatsen, a former employee of Frank Lloyd Wright who popularized the Prairie Style in Seattle during the first few decades of this century. Jongeward's house features several Prairie-style attributes: a low-pitched, broad-hipped roof, horizontal wood siding topped by a band of stucco, and a row of sash windows placed directly under the eaves.

The house boasts breathtaking vistas of downtown Seattle, Mount Rainier, Elliott Bay, and both the Cascade and Olympic Mountain ranges. Inside, the scenery is vintage

Jongeward: elegant and refined, but without the stuffy trappings that beleaguer many formal homes. The designer maintains the light and contemporary mood by keeping the "bones" simple and embellishing the surroundings.

Jongeward approached the house like a blank canvas, commissioning artist Leo Adams to create a mural on the walls of the living room and entry hall. Adams's supple, sinuous ribbons of color recall the desert hills of his native eastern Washington. The swirling earthtone bands help break down the living room's boxy proportions while uniting the thirty-foot room into a unified whole.

Jongeward didn't stop at the walls. Adams also contributed to the library ceiling, a trompe l'oeil distorted checker-

board in the style of Victor Vasarely. "It was supposed to form a dome but it doesn't, unless you have two glasses of wine and end up under the table," says the designer, laughing.

The house's bare oak floors were painted in modified sunbursts and geometrics by artist Larry Launceford. The graphics help define seating areas while recalling the classic inlaid marble floors of Italian villas. "I use a lot of craftspeople in my work," says Jongeward. "I always have. I think what I do is honest, and it's an honest thing to use the craftspeople of this area. It feels right to me."

Jongeward seeks the same honesty in her furnishings, favoring clean, uncontrived, monochromatic pieces that

A chinoiserie desk from the early-nineteenth century stands in the foyer atop Larry Launceford's painted oak floor (FAR LEFT).

The floor is adorned with a modified sunburst design inspired by the inlaid marble floors of Italian villas. Doors to the living room are inset with screens to help separate the rooms (MIDDLE LEFT).

Painted canvas covers the walls of the foyer and the doors into the library (ABOVE). A Shigaraki jar stands on a plexiglass pedestal in front of a Japanese scroll from the Edo period.

**T**he former dining room has been converted into a library (NEAR RIGHT), which is decorated with a Vasarely-style trompe l'oeil ceiling. The owner says it only resembles a dome if you've imbibed too much and end up under the table.

**B**ooks on art and design crowd the shelves of the library. A painting by Alberto Burri hangs above a Japanese folding makeup mirror, standing figure, and black lacquer box. The chair is a Chippendale reproduction (MIDDLE RIGHT).

**P**re-Columbian statues share shelf space in the library with a framed piece of Coptic textile and an assortment of netsukes—intricate ivory carvings used as fasteners on kimono sashes (BELOW).

**T**ravel mementos and gifts from protégés embellish the library (FAR RIGHT). The owner attributes the room's depth and richness to layering, rather than any set decorating plan.

▲▲▲▲▲▲▲▲▲▲▲▲▲▲▲▲▲▲▲▲▲▲▲▲▲▲▲

**A** Louis XIII table sits in front of a Breton cupboard in the kitchen (FAR LEFT). Once used for ecclesiastical purposes, the cupboard now serves as a liquor cabinet.

**P**art work space, part museum, the kitchen is home to a host of international collectibles, including a Thai cabbage grater in the shape of a rabbit, Italian cannisters, and eighteenth-century blue and white china from Canton (LEFT).

complement the patterned floors, walls, and ceiling. Many of the pieces are of her own design: armless chairs and loveseats (the designer claims that arms just break up a room's visual flow), a dining table made entirely of glass, and a coffee table with a brass base and Plexiglas top, which doubles as a tray—another one of the designer's signatures.

Even traditional pieces have a pared-down look. Louis XVI chairs have been stripped to a pale patina and upholstered in the same beige canvas used throughout. "I always have canvas on my furniture," says Jongeward. "I love it. Before canvas, I used linen. It's simple."

The fireplace mantel, which extends the width of the living room, is made from two sheets of dark glass inset with a narrow band of brass. Glass frames the firebox and covers the hearth, as well.

"Because I'm bombarded with form and color and texture in my work, I have to have a quiet place when I come home," says the designer of her predominantly putty-colored house.

"I like color that is quite grayed and restrained, and that's what I've always used. I think it takes advantage of the light—it becomes part of it. You have the same feeling outside as when you step inside. It's just . . . a mellowness."

Jongeward embellishes the house's cool, tailored furnishings with antiques and accessories collected on her travels throughout the world. The designer favors simple forms imbued with rich colors and textures: timeworn Japanese urns; African pottery, carvings, and bracelets; shards of Southwest pottery piled upon a small tribal chair; Japanese hairpieces arranged atop a lacquer tray; a Queen Anne chinoiserie cabinet fitted with gleaming brass hardware.

A tiny breakfast room is home to a pair of Chippendale chairs and an eighteenth-century Sheraton settee. The tapestry above it once hung at William Randolph Hearst's San Simeon.

The adjacent kitchen is as much museum as workplace, from the Cantonese porcelain adorning the walls (the pieces

The designer-owner considers the use of local artists and craftspeople a natural accompaniment to home design in the Northwest. The wall murals in her living room were painted by artist Leo Adams, who drew his inspiration from the hills of his native Yakima, Washington. Simple canvas upholstery and a black glass fireplace surround complement Adams's creation.

The painted walls and floor provide a lively backdrop for the living room's simple, neutral furnishings. The coffee table designed by the owner features a removable Plexiglas top. Painted boulders—a recent addition to the wall mural—frame a Queen Anne chinoiserie cabinet (TOP RIGHT).

The owner designed the upholstered bench, which doubles as a side table with the addition of a Plexiglas tray (BOTTOM RIGHT). On it sits a pair of nineteenth-century Japanese hair ornaments, Italian and African bracelets, an African fish, and a Chinese jade adz.

were used as ship ballast crossing the Pacific) to the circa-1800 Breton cupboard, the Tibetan teapot, and the Bennington pottery crowding the countertop.

Jongeward's favorite retreat is the library, which was originally designed as a dining room and is still used for that purpose on occasion. The cozy, cluttered room is lined from floor to ceiling with built-in bookshelves. Even one of the doors to the room is a bookshelf, which pivots on hinges to shut the room off from the front hall. Volumes on art and architecture crowd every corner, sharing space with a cornucopia of collectibles ranging from pre-Columbian figures to Japanese lacquer to French art deco. Many of the pieces she collected herself; others are gifts from her "kids"—the young designers she has taken under her wing over the years.

Jongeward moved to Seattle during World War II when her serviceman husband was shipped overseas. "When I saw the Northwest it was a total wonder," says the designer. "Growing up in the Midwest I had never been really aware of contemporary art and architecture, and here it was!"

Despite her lack of formal design training, she landed a position as a "Home Planner" in the interior design department at a leading Seattle department store. She worked for a succession of prestigious firms before striking out on her own in the early sixties.

Her career has given her little time to work on her own house. In fact, the present design was whipped together in a couple of months back in 1971 when Jongeward volunteered the house for a Seattle Art Museum architectural tour. The day before the tour she and her assistants worked through the night, applying the last coat of paint just moments before the first visitors crossed the threshold.

The house was the talk of the tour. "People were startled," recalls Jongeward. "I guess it was ahead of its time. Today, people are used to graphics on floors and chairs without arms, but then they weren't."

Jongeward has changed little about the house in the ensuing years, allowing the layering of time to add richness and depth to her original scheme. What stands today is not the product of planning, but the result of uncanny instinct and unfailing taste—those attributes that epitomize the oft-mentioned, but seldom-seen, quality known as style.

The timeworn patina of Japanese storage jars contrast with the tailored simplicity of the owner's armless seating units.

Shards of Southwest pottery are piled atop a small African chair on the living room table (RIGHT). The bracelets are also African.

# City Beach House

## EAST

## MEETS WEST IN

## AN ARCHITECT'S

## WEST SEATTLE HOME

Images of Japanese architecture and American beach houses combine in this West Seattle house. The broad, low roof, exposed rafters, and transparent walls suggest the Orient, while the shingled exterior and low profile recall seaside cottages of yesteryear. Heat-reflecting glass helps keep the interior cool. The house was elevated above the beach to alleviate any threat of damage from the tide.

The weathered hull of an overturned rowboat (LEFT) lies dormant in the beach grass. The house overlooks Puget Sound, the armlike extension of the Pacific that skirts Seattle's shores. Vashon Island and the Kitsap Peninsula are visible in the distance. Often called "the birthplace of Seattle," West Seattle was home to the area's first settlement in 1851. In a show of optimism, the pioneers christened the settlement "New York," to which the Chinook Indians rejoindered *Alki*, meaning "someday." A stretch of West Seattle shoreline still bears that Indian name.

**T**ransparent walls of glass link interior and exterior in this living room view. The Vashon Island ferry terminal is visible in the distance. Lloyd Loom wicker chairs flank a 1920s bamboo table used for casual dining. Nineteenth-century Japanese storage boxes serve as end tables alongside the customized sofa and wicker chairs, one of which was picked up at a local swap meet.

**W**ith its glittering lakes and miles of saltwater shoreline, Seattle offers ample opportunity to live by the water while enjoying the convenience of the city. This "decadent" combination has been exploited to perfection in the house architect George Suyama designed for himself and his wife Kim. Situated in West Seattle, just fifteen minutes from the center of the city, the house celebrates sophisticated city living without forsaking the casualness and tranquillity that are the hallmarks of waterfront life.

Although it was the first house that George and Kim Suyama had ever built from scratch, they still had a fairly good idea of what they wanted. During their first decade of marriage alone the couple had purchased, remodeled, and sold no fewer than five houses.

Says Kim Suyama, "In the process of all those remodelings, we've gone through a lot of different living scenarios and really refined what we like and how we live, the kinds of spaces that we needed and the kinds of spaces that we didn't need."

In designing the house, Suyama was careful to respect the traditions of the beach house without becoming subservient to them. The wide, low-pitched roof, stained shingle siding, breeze-embracing casement windows, and woodsy interior pay tribute to waterfront homes of yore. But these attributes are balanced by such citified touches as a strong vertical orientation, open floor plan, and innovative use of materials. In lesser hands, the combination might have seemed somewhat schizophrenic. Here, they conspire to bring out the best of both worlds.

In refining his design, Suyama tried to eliminate as many elements as possible without sacrificing the house's basic form. The architect carefully cut away at walls and ceilings, creating gaps and interior windows that allow light, sound, and views to pass from space to space with liquid ease. He pierced the center of the home with a thirty-foot light well containing a sandblasted steel stairway. Skeletal banisters frame the stair's oak treads, which seem to float between the two floors of the house.

Floor-to-ceiling windows along the west wall offer unobstructed views of sand, sky, and water. The rhythmic fenes-

**91**

The courtyard patio (RIGHT) functions like an outdoor room, offering privacy and protection from the winds blowing off the water. French doors on either side lead to the dining room (left) and studio (right).

Joseph Goldberg's encaustic painting hangs in the dining room above a collection of early-nineteenth-century saki bottles (MIDDLE RIGHT). The panel supporting the painting conceals an alcove that will one day house an upright piano.

tration of the glass helps frame the scenery, while the natural slope down to the beach preserves the couple's privacy from inquisitive beachcombers. Offshore, a parade of ferryboats ply the waters of Puget Sound, their forms silhouetted against the sun-dappled waves and blue-gray mountains.

In keeping with the beach house spirit, the owners have forsaken formality in favor of creature comfort. A warming wood stove, a wall of books, and comfortable, casual furnishings add to the living room's amiable ambience. Beiges, browns, and greens—"the Northwest colors," the owner calls them—dominate the 2,500-square-foot interior. Cherished old boat models, a commodious tansu chest topped with corpulent Hotei dolls, and eighteenth-century Seto horseye plates add a touch of timelessness to the room's contemporary lines.

Old sake bottles line the steps to the dining room, which is dominated by a sturdy ash table built to Suyama's specifications and joined together with wooden pegs in the traditional Japanese manner. The kitchen just beyond is divided into two parts: the "public" portion, open to the dining room and out-

fitted with a commercial gas range and food preparation area; and the "private" portion, featuring appliances, cleanup facilities, and storage. The split operation allows the owners to socialize with guests as they cook, without exposing their company to the mess and clutter that often accompany a meal.

French doors surround the courtyard patio, where the owners may enjoy the elements in privacy without being exposed to westerly winds or the eyes of onlookers. A wood stove warms the adjacent studio, which will eventually have a drawing board for George Suyama and a knitting machine for Kim Suyama, and will double as a guest room for overnight visitors.

The house accommodates soirees for 100 and evenings for two with equal ease, thanks to a series of recessed alcoves bordering the living room, dining room, and kitchen, which free up floor space downstairs. While some of the alcoves are fully exposed, like those containing the living room bookcases and the kitchen range, others hide behind sliding shojilike panels of fir framed in cedar. The panels glide back and forth, revealing or concealing the contents of

**T**he oversized compartments lead the owner to believe that the tansu chest in the living room may once have held bedding. The piece, made from keyaki, a Japanese hardwood, dates from around 1860, as do the Hotei dolls on top, whose protruding stomachs and enlarged ear lobes signify wealth and happiness. Seto horseye plates from about 1820 lean against a basket of horsetails found in Eastern Washington. A painting by Alden Mason hangs upon a sliding wood panel that conceals a home entertainment system in the other side of the alcove.

**A** 130-year-old mizuya (kitchen storage cupboard) stands in the alcove adjoining the dining area (TOP RIGHT). These recessed niches expand each room visually, while freeing up floor space for circulation.

**T**he "public" portion of the kitchen is outfitted with a commercial range inset within a tiled alcove (BOTTOM RIGHT). Ribbed aluminum grease filters, like those found in restaurants, line the back side of the customized range hood. The hanging tube light is a fluorescent fixture that was retrofitted with incandescent bulbs.

**T**he sandblasted steel staircase acts like a giant piece of sculpture dividing the dining area from the living room (FAR RIGHT). Craftsman Dale Brotherton built the ash dining table to the owner's specifications, assembling it with pegs in the traditional Japanese manner. The whole table can be taken apart in a matter of minutes. Brotherton used no sandpaper—every surface is hand-planed.

94

A Danish wood stove divides the living and dining areas (LEFT). Wood is stored in an old copper basin. Level changes, low partitions, and slender columns help to break up the open plan while preserving views to the water.

The thirty-foot light well (ABOVE) is pierced by a sandblasted steel staircase and exposed flue, which helps warm the 2,500-square-foot interior. The walls and ceilings were peeled away to create a complex arrangement of intersecting volumes and planes, which all but disguise the house's simple boxlike form.

each alcove, thereby altering the dimensions and functions of the adjoining space.

According to Suyama, the idea was sparked by the Japanese notion of creating spaces within spaces. The architect, a third-generation American of Japanese descent, derives much of his inspiration from his ancestral home. "I think the Oriental influence is such a perfect fit with this region," he says. "The water, the mountains, the forest— everything fits."

The home's slatted spruce ceiling was modeled after those found in Japan, as was the commodious soaking tub that dominates the top-floor master bath. Windows alongside the tub overlook the courtyard patio below. When opened, the cool breeze sends billowing clouds of steam dancing across the surface of the water to the soothing accompaniment of waves lapping against the beach. A Jap-

anese lantern hangs alongside the tub over the vanity, which is made from poured-in-place concrete coated with a wax finish for a natural, stonelike appearance.

The master bedroom across the hall is divided into three parts: a tall central portion containing the bed and sitting area, and two dressing areas on either side. Overhead timbers frame the bed like a four-poster, with roll-down shades providing additional privacy. In the summer, the bedroom windows swing open, turning the room into a semienclosed sitting porch. When the weather turns foul, a narrow air vent in the bedroom wall allows the soothing sound of the seashore to penetrate the interior.

Antiques have always played an integral role in Suyama's designs. This is no less true in his own home, where every tabletop and tansu is laden with treasures. While some pieces came from antique stores, many others were found at

A steer skull surveys the master bath (FAR LEFT), which features a poured-in-place concrete countertop and custom-spun stainless steel sink. The architect-homeowner designed the light fixtures, which are showcase bulbs suspended from wires. The wall at right stops short of the ceiling, enhancing the feeling of openness and flexibility that is key to a Japanese home.

A Japanese-style soaking tub (MIDDLE LEFT) overlooks the courtyard patio. When the windows are open, bathers can listen to the sound of the waves lapping the beach while billowing clouds of steam dance across the surface of the water. The Japanese garden lantern illuminates a nineteenth-century backpack, a sumo doll dressed in red pantaloons, and a glass piece by Dale Chihuly. The painting is by Gaylen Hansen.

The master bedroom (LEFT) consists of a high-ceilinged central portion flanked by his-and-her dressing areas. Roll-down screens hang from the overhead beam, suggesting a latter-day four-poster. The bedspread is made from old futon fabric decorated with a seaweed design.

swap meets and thrift shops. "I do not like going to showrooms and buying things," says the architect. "I would rather build something or find something. I like the quest, I like the satisfaction of the solution, and I like the individuality of it—the fact that nobody else has that."

Some pieces are clustered on ceiling-hugging ledges positioned over the front entry hall and bathroom. The idea was inspired by the overhead spans found in old post-and-beam Japanese houses. Most of the Japanese antiques date from the Edo and Meiji periods of the mid-nineteenth century. The humble, folk-art pieces blend beautifully with the warm expanses of wood and neutral, earthtone color scheme. But Suyama isn't afraid to mix periods and locales. An antique Japanese horsehair rain hat looks perfectly at home alongside a fanciful painted snake from the American Southwest and a garage sale mirror draped with Peruvian dolls and

dime store jewelry. "I've decided that if you like something, you just get it and it will go together," Suyama says assuredly.

By illuminating individual objects instead of entire rooms, Suyama fills the interior with a soft, diffuse light that accentuates the layering of the space. Many of the fixtures are of his own creation, like the entry hall lights fashioned from outdoor spotlights and the futuristic vanity lights made from suspended showcase bulbs.

The house's success can be measured best, however, not by the new ideas it espouses, but by the traditions it upholds. For instead of creating a monument to himself, Suyama has chosen to learn from those who came before him. By respecting proven principles of function, light, color, and comfort, the architect has created a home of both timeless beauty and enduring practicality.

# Floating Homes

### CREATIVE LIVING

### ON FIVE

### SEATTLE HOUSEBOATS

**H**ouseboat docks line the shores of Seattle's Lake Union, an in-city oasis shared by industry, maritime interests, government research vessels, and recreational users.

**F**or years, the owners' float was home to a railroad boxcar. Then, in the mid-seventies, the structure was removed and the present home was built (LEFT).

Houseboaters live a life most of us just dream about. Caressed by the gentle lapping of the waves, serenaded by the cry of geese bobbing outside the window, dazzled by the pastel reflection of sunsets upon the water, theirs is a world of intoxicating sights, sounds, and sensations.

The residents of Seattle's 450 floating homes live within a few miles of downtown on Lake Union and adjoining Portage Bay. Huddled on weatherbeaten docks projecting out from the shore, the houseboats are as varied as the people who live within them. Some homes are little more than shacks—their paint blistering, their windows covered with curtains fashioned from old pillowcases. Others have been remodeled to resemble quaint chalets or Victorian cottages. Still others are soaring contemporaries with sheer cedar walls and dramatically angled roofs.

In the summer, flowers spill from porch-front planters and hang in fragrant clusters from the eaves. Corkscrew willows cling tenaciously to their scant allotments of soil, sometimes seeming to emerge from the water itself. Cats loll in flowerboxes or bound between float and dock, tempting fate for a chance caress from a passerby.

Unlike European houseboats, which travel under their own propulsion, Seattle's floating homes are designed to stay in one place. For years, the structures were supported on floats made from cedar logs. As the wood became waterlogged, new layers of logs were rolled underneath. Over time, a houseboat could rest atop as many as fifteen feet of logs!

As cedar grew scarce in the 1950s, steel drums were filled with air and used for added flotation. In recent years, houseboats have been constructed atop concrete platforms filled with pockets of Styrofoam.

Sometimes less than an arm's length separates one house from another, but the proximity inspires friendliness and a protective feeling among neighbors. Some houseboat owners don't even lock their doors, since strangers can rarely approach undetected and the avenues of escape are limited.

Today's houseboat population runs the gamut from artists to professionals to retirees. Most are attracted to the floating life by the romance and excitement of living someplace just a

**H**ouseboat owners are privy to a constantly changing panorama of sights and sounds. From their window seat (LEFT), Patton and Major can cheer the Tuesday evening "Duck Dodge" sailboat races, watch seaplanes take off and land, or admire the Fourth of July fireworks exploding overhead.

**T**he stripped pine dining room set (TOP) was made locally, as was the artist-designed fish tank behind it. The top half of the Dutch door is hinged within the door frame, so that it can swing open even when the rest of the door is closed.

**T**he two-story living room (ABOVE) features cedar walls and a warming wood stove.

little bit different from the next fellow. The pride and spirit of camaraderie they share has seen the houseboat community through its fair share of stormy waters.

Houseboats first appeared on Puget Sound nearly 100 years ago. Seattle's earliest houseboaters were fishermen who tied their boats or floating shacks to the piers and railroad trestles bordering downtown Seattle on Elliott Bay. These resourceful souls scavenged building materials and built upon retired barges, boat hulls, or log rafts. In 1908 the Seattle Health Department banned houseboats from Elliott Bay, claiming they were unsanitary. The Health Department conveniently overlooked the fact that the city's sewers were allowed to run untreated into the same waters.

In the early years of this century the houseboat population shifted to the Duwamish River, a working waterway feeding into Elliott Bay. Laborers toiling in the lumber mills along the river retired at night to the floating shacks tied up along the shore. They were a tough, independent lot, a far cry from the society crowd establishing themselves on nearby Lake Washington around the same time. The Lake Washington residents built elegant houseboats equipped with all the latest conveniences, including electricity, telephones, and indoor plumbing.

"Hospitality is a byword among those who live on the lake," trumpeted *The Seattle Post-Intelligencer*, which went on to talk of informal lunches, late-evening spreads, and musical soirees along the shore.

But the paper changed its tune three years later when it printed a harsh assessment of these denizens of the deep. "They're a lazy crew—the houseboat mariners," asserted the paper in a 1908 story. "They idle away precious hours, forgetting that the real object of life is to make money, and that time is money." It was the first of countless attacks houseboat owners would have to endure in the ensuing decades.

Lake Union was the last body of water to be settled by the houseboats. Originally known by the Indian name "Tenas Chuck," or "Little Water," the lake earned its present moniker in 1854 from Seattle founding father Thomas Mercer, who must have foreseen the system of waterways that would link the lake with Lake Washington to the east and Puget Sound to the west some sixty-three years later.

**A**rchitect Lasse K. Jaakola designed the floating home owned by Lanny and Pat Carver (TOP LEFT), which rests upon a concrete pad filled with pockets of Styrofoam. Projecting bays and recessed porches help break up the boxiness that often results from trying to stretch maximum space out of a twenty-four by forty-five-foot base. Gangplanks accommodate changes in water height.

**T**he rooftop deck (BOTTOM LEFT) is equipped with a built-in sink and refrigerator, as well as a gas-flamed barbecue, purchased after two charcoal ones toppled overboard. The temperature is usually warmer over the water, and the clouds often break even when it's cloudy on shore. At Christmastime, the owners are treated to parades of decorated boats and canoes filled with carolers.

105

**O**versized windows in the Carvers' living room (TOP RIGHT) let in views of the lake, while glass block insets mask the surrounding deck. The cabinet over the fireplace conceals the TV, freeing up precious floor space and keeping clutter away from the windows. In the summer, a cooling breeze blows off the water. In winter, a heat pump draws warmth from the surrounding water to heat the house.

**T**he owners' tugboat style cabin cruiser, *Brigadoon* (BOTTOM RIGHT), waits by the back deck. Houseboat living means "free" moorage and no more trips to the marina.

**A**lthough narrow at the bottom, the staircase (FAR RIGHT) bulges out at the landing to permit room for passing. Flat railings were deemed lighter and less imposing than round ones, helping to preserve those all-important views. A built-in wine rack at right takes advantage of what would otherwise be wasted space.

In order to finance the Alaska-Yukon-Pacific Exposition of 1909, the state legislature sold off private plat lots around the perimeter of Lake Union. Property owners rented the underwater land for houseboat moorages, figuring there was little else that could be done with it. The homes that began appearing on the lake were usually built from found materials or wood appropriated from the nearby lumber mills. Small, rectangular homes of one or two rooms were the norm, with many featuring "sprung" (rounded) roofs, which were easier to construct than conventional peaked roofs. You can still recognize houseboats from this period by these distinctive roof lines.

The First World War gave a boost to Seattle's economy and the houseboat population. Between 1915 and 1919 approximately 300 houseboats were built on the Duwamish River and the two lakes to meet the demand for inexpensive housing for workers. But as the number of houseboats soared, their reputation grew increasingly unsavory. Radical "Wobblies" (members of the International Workers of the World), prostitutes, and bootleggers found an insular, accepting environment on the water.

Bootleggers became especially active after 1914, the year Washington State went dry. The waterways are rife with tales of home breweries and stills, and of the inevitable raids in which gallons of hooch were hoisted overboard. So much alcohol wound up in the drink that old-timers swear you could get a buzz just walking along the shore. Also at this time, prostitution flourished along the water in both private homes and floating speakeasies.

One longtime houseboat owner, Dick Wagner, holds fond memories of his early houseboating days, when he rented a floating home with two friends for fifty dollars a month. The fee included free nightly jam sessions provided by his jazz-playing moorage owner. "I came from New Jersey, where all of the waterfront anywhere was either used commercially, was a corporate headquarters, or was owned by some rich people," says Wagner. "Here, not only could you buy a houseboat for next to nothing, but people that were living on next to nothing could live on the water."

The houseboat population swelled during the Depression as members of the working class, desperate for cheap housing, set up "temporary" quarters on the water. However,

with the return of prosperity, public tolerance for this alternative way of life diminished, as did the houseboat population. Between the 1930s and the early 1960s the number of floating homes plummeted from over 2,000 to just 540. Development had displaced the houseboats along the Duwamish, while Lake Washington houseboats were outlawed on the grounds that they detracted from the lake's prime residential property. Lake Union moorages dwindled in the wake of development and local legislation.

Government and civic groups continued to label houseboats an environmental hazard, since their waste flowed untreated into the water. Finally, in the mid-sixties, the city built a sewer around Lake Union and declared that houseboats would have to hook up or perish. Although the need for the sewer was evident, the ruling proved to be a death knell for the scores of houseboats that either couldn't be plumbed or were simply not worth the expense.

For the rest of the houseboat community, the sewers marked the dawn of a new age. Suddenly, houseboats were ecologically and financially sound investments. Moorage rates increased to pay for the sewer connections. The higher

costs drove away low-income residents and attracted a middle-class crowd that took a greater interest in protecting their investment. "Until we had the sewers nobody bothered getting too serious about tying up their houseboats," says Dick Wagner. "There'd always be a few floating around at the end of a storm. The harbor police would gather them up and push them back where they belonged."

Banks took notice of the newfound respectability and began financing houseboat purchases for the first time. In the late sixties and early seventies, forty-six houseboats were built—the biggest surge in houseboat construction since the 1940s. For the first time houseboats were designed for aesthetics as well as keeping the rain out. Multistory houseboats with angular roofs and trim, cedar-clad exteriors began popping up on Portage Bay, setting a standard for floating-home design for decades to come.

The houseboat population shifted from students and bohemians to doctors, lawyers, and university professors. Gone were the days when a rising executive would give his employer a phony address for fear of anyone discovering he lived on the water.

Lanny and Pat Carver are typical of the new breed of houseboat owners: vibrant, active professionals drawn to houseboating's blend of cosmopolitan convenience and country casualness. Their custom-designed, two-story, cedar-sided contemporary rests along Roanoke Reef, a tony development of like-styled houseboats erected on Lake Union just a stone's throw from where William E. Boeing built and tested his first airplanes back in 1915. The Carvers' spacious, flowing interior features glass block, deco-inspired furniture, and an Olympic-sized walk-in closet (an occupational hazard of couples employed in the wholesale clothing business).

"We'd never move," says Pat Carver. "When you come home you feel like you're coming to a vacation house. And you're ten minutes from work!"

Avid boaters, the Carvers enjoy piling their belongings into the thirty-seven-foot cabin cruiser moored alongside their houseboat and taking off on an excursion. No more tiresome trips to the marina.

Richard Patton and Cathi Major live in a woodsy, shingle-clad houseboat across Lake Union from the Carvers. The

▴▴▴▴▴▴▴▴▴▴▴▴▴▴▴▴▴▴▴▴▴▴▴▴▴▴▴▴▴▴▴▴▴▴▴▴

**T**he Carver home's art deco aura continues in the master bedroom (LEFT), which is outfitted with a thirties' rattan chair and a rattan bed. The doorway at right leads to a tiny deck.

**T**wo separate houseboats were joined in the 1930s to form the present houseboat owned by Rob Anglin and Peggy Hackney (BELOW LEFT). You can still see where the "sprung" roof of one meets the gable roof of the other.

**A**nglin enclosed the front porch to expand the living room and create a nursery (BELOW MIDDLE).

**T**he interior was opened up to the roofline, allowing construction of a loft overlooking the living room (BELOW RIGHT). The hallway at left runs the length of the house, allowing Hackney, a dancer, to practice her warmup runs in the morning.

**T**he gentle rocking of the waves helps lull one to sleep. It's like sleeping on a waterbed without the water (TOP RIGHT).

**G**lossy black cabinets add an elegant touch to Anglin's diminutive bathroom (BOTTOM RIGHT), which is brightened by a skylight over the tub.

**T**he owner saved the existing kitchen cabinets (FAR RIGHT) and fitted them with new wire glass cabinet doors, back-painted a gloss black for a contemporary look. The French doors open out to the deck.

110

original owner built the home back in the mid-seventies. Patton and Major have spruced the place up with cushy, colorful seating, a pillow-lined window seat, and a neo-Wrightian dining set made locally from stripped pine. "It's not like a boat," says Major of her 1,250-square-foot home. "It's like a condominium—but unique."

Rob Anglin and Peggy Hackney agreed to declare their kitchen a "purple-free" zone after painting the rest of their houseboat a pungent periwinkle. The quaint, one-story structure was formed from two separate houseboats back in the 1930s. Anglin, an architect, opened up the interior, recycling parts when possible and improvising when not: his wall sconces are made from sheets of watercolor paper framed in old door casing and fitted with refrigerator bulbs.

While often less expensive than landed homes, houseboats are also a lot smaller, averaging between 800 and 1,200 square feet. While about half of all moorages are owned cooperatively by the houseboat residents, the other half of the population must pay a monthly moorage fee that can range from 225 dollars to 350 dollars, depending on the dock and the houseboat's location on the dock.

Strict rules govern the size and height of floating homes in order to prevent crowding and preserve sunlight and views. Inside space must be organized with shiplike efficiency. Since there are no basements or attics on houseboats, storage space is carved out of any unused area, like the space under a staircase or beneath a bed.

The lack of space makes decorating a challenge. "You can't just go out and buy a bunch of furniture," says Pat Carver. "If you don't like it, you can't move it to another room. Things have to fit—there's just no moving it around."

Houseboats are also very sensitive to weight. Heavy accumulations of snow on the roof have been known to sink older houseboats. If furniture isn't distributed evenly throughout the interior, the heavy ends will become submerged. When this happens, Styrofoam chunks have to be added underneath the house to buoy it up. Architect Greg Maxwell remodeled his Depression-era houseboat three times during the course of eight years. Each time, he had to juggle the flotation underneath to accommodate his grand piano. Moving the piano onto the houseboat presented its

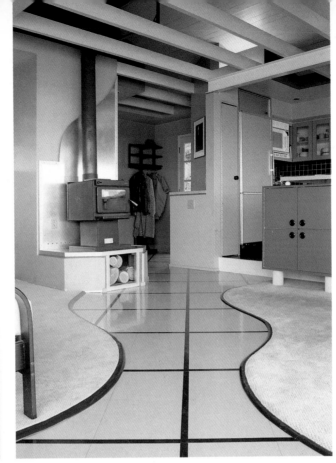

**P**orcelain enamel steel alternates with beveled wood siding on the exterior of the houseboat owned by Greg Maxwell (FAR TOP LEFT). The black borders around the windows act as a highlight, providing a contemporary update on traditional window moldings.

**V**ariegated ceiling planes add visual and spatial interest to the compact living room (TOP MIDDLE LEFT). Each time the piano is moved, Styrofoam floats have to be added or repositioned under the house to accommodate the shift in weight.

**T**he tile floor (TOP LEFT) mimics the grid of the exterior steel panels. Sinuous curves in the carpeting and stove-back temper the strong geometry. The Maxwells opened up the ceiling and exposed the rafters to lend a greater sense of spaciousness to the 850-square-foot house. The owner designed the custom cabinetry, which conceals a TV set (FAR BOTTOM LEFT). The counter above rests on a pool ball.

**T**he compact kitchen (BOTTOM MIDDLE LEFT) blends Eurostyle sleekness with shipshape efficiency. Meals are eaten at the built-in breakfast bar.

**S**unlight floods the high-tech bathroom (BOTTOM LEFT), which is fitted with a Scandinavian washbasin and wire-glass shower enclosure.

113

own problems: the aging dock nearly sank under the movers' feet.

Maxwell (a Pisces who sheepishly traces his love of houseboating to his astrological orientation) made an offer on the squat, rectangular house the first day he set foot on it in 1980. Today the home bears little resemblance to that dark, fifty-year-old shack. Maxwell replaced two living room walls with sliding glass doors that open the interior completely to the deck and surrounding water. A grid of porcelain enamel steel panels embrace the exterior, while inside the grid continues in a bold diagonal sweep of gray and black tile. Maxwell counterpoints the strong lines with sinuous piano curves in the carpet and ceiling, which is eroded away in areas to reveal the structural elements underneath. Accents

of teal and raspberry add vigor to the coolly neutral palette.

Artist Thom Laz has watched the changes of the last two decades from the funky, cluttered houseboat he purchased back in 1968 for 550 dollars. Since then, Laz has added onto his one-room shack with improvisatory abandon. Leaded glass windows sparkle with sunlight, projecting splinters of light into the cluttered corners of the art-filled interior. Books bulge from every shelf, while crystals, carvings, and chimes hang above the comfortable, castaway furnishings.

"I wish all the houseboats were still funky," says Laz. "I wish this place was still worth 550 dollars, and I wish I was still paying thirty dollars a month for moorage. But times change, and you've got to roll with the punches or you get knocked out."

**A**n exit sign, a collection of sunglasses, and a watch-toting gargoyle hang over the Hobbit-sized front door (TOP ROW LEFT) of Thom Laz's houseboat.

**A** Naugahyde child's chair (TOP ROW MIDDLE LEFT) sits before a 1926 wood stove manufactured in Seattle. Thom carved the mahagony head on top.

**A** bevy of Balinese flying dragons hang amidst a canopy of philodendron and ivy in the bed-sitting area adjacent to the deck (TOP ROW MIDDLE RIGHT). Moorages located at the end of the dock, like this one, are highly prized and highly priced, since they offer unobstructed views, ample sunlight, and maximum privacy.

**P**ots and pans dominate the airspace over the kitchen (TOP ROW RIGHT). The skylight opens for added ventilation.

**B**y raising the roof a few feet, it was possible to create a bedroom loft with a panoramic view of the lake and the Seattle skyline (BOTTOM ROW LEFT).

**T**he framed prints lining the kitchen wall (BOTTOM ROW RIGHT) are hinged at the top. They lift up to reveal pantry storage shelves.

**L**az has added onto the house bit by bit over the last two decades, turning a one-room shack into a rambling accumulation of nooks and crannies, each embellished with the artist's own personal touch (LEFT).

# Indian Ancestry

## A MOSAIC

## OF LAND AND LIFE

## IN EASTERN

## WASHINGTON

**T**he house sits on a gentle knoll, part of the Ahtanum Ridge.

**A** bit of ribbon, a braided string, autumn leaves—all humble materials—combine to create the illusion of a Florentine masterpiece (LEFT).

The Yakima Valley, its tawny carpet of sun-drenched fields reflecting the brilliant light of eastern Washington, is part of the great Columbia plateau, which stretches across 180 miles of nearly treeless land. Once a semiarid wasteland, this irrigated farm-country yields some of the richest harvests in the nation, all due to a marvelous feat of ingenuity and engineering: the Grand Coulee Dam. Harnessing the power and productivity of the Columbia River, this million-acre tract of lava beds and dry canyon makes Washington a leading producer of wheat, dry peas, hops, potatoes, cattle, and soft fruits. Bite into a Red Delicious apple, and odds are it was grown in eastern Washington.

Although ponderosa pine and other timber grow in mountain foothills and the valleys, when contrasted with western Washington, this plateau often resembles a moonscape. The summers are hot and dry with temperatures hovering around ninety degrees, and the winters can be bitterly cold.

The Yakima Ridge rises easterly out of the Cascade Mountain foothills, a formidable series of parched hills that caution motorists: "No gas for twenty-nine miles." The hills finally give way to the valley, a rich tapestry of gold, brown, ochre, purple, and gray-green. Nearly one and a half million acres of the valley is owned by the Yakima Indian Nation, whose reservation covers some of the richest land in eastern Washington, a vast and incredibly diverse ecosystem of fishing streams, timber, cattleland, orchards, and farmland.

The Yakima Indians, who first breathed life into this valley 1000 years ago, negotiated a treaty with the U.S. Government in 1855, reserving 1.2 million acres for their nation out of the original 12 million acres of ancestral homeland. In lieu of taxes they ceded the remainder for all time. Land allotments were given to each Indian family, and today much of

A bullet hole-riddled appliance (TOP RIGHT), found in the fields, is snipped and mitred to form a fireplace surround.

Small objects, a Japanese bowl filled with dried weeds, a whale bone, a lily, sit on a sponged plywood round (RIGHT). The careful placement of a chair is a common tool among designers who sense an almost human relationship between chairs and juxtaposed objects.

**A** stretched charcoal blanket covers the living room wall space, providing the perfect backdrop for a Leo Adams painting. Casually placed Louis XV chairs sit on a painted floorcloth.

that land has been leased to non-Indian farmers. Although the land has been put to good use, farming increases the demand for limited water, and the free flowing streams, so important to Indian salmon fishing, are diminishing. Once again, the Indians are confronted with the age-old struggle of preserving their traditional and sacred way of living in concert with the land.

Leo Adams, a painter, designer, and Yakima Indian, carries the sense of this land in his soul. Tied to this country by his ethnic origin and his keen understanding of color, texture, and light, his home and art give eloquent testimony to the grandeur of the valley. Located on Yakima Indian Reservation land, the house sits in a field surrounded by orchards, pasture, and wheat and alfalfa fields. Much of the vegetation,

such as wild grass, yarrow, sagebrush, greasewood, and wildflowers, has found its way into Adams's house in the form of giant bouquets, wall sculptures, and furniture. A bundle of dried willow can be just as easily transformed into a table base as into a headboard. Antiques sit gracefully on painted plywood floors, and sheets of corrugated metal climb ten feet up the wall to form a backdrop for oil barrels stuffed with dried weeds.

Born to a tribal councilman and raised in the Yakima Valley, Adams has had precious little formal art or design education. At an early age he showed a keen sensitivity to his environment, bringing home bits and pieces of the landscape and incorporating them into his play space. "If I saw that it was beautiful, I had it near me for a while and learned from it.

**S**inuously carved armoire doors lend an air of classicism to this living room mélange of found objects and traditional pieces (FAR LEFT). The chandelier, crafted of simple rope, has all the character of its crystal cousin.

**A** Louis XVI console (LEFT) is created from uncut corduroy, dipped in paint, then twisted and tied around a simple shape. The mirror is likewise constructed from rusted metal and weathered plywood, then detailed with Oriental brushstrokes.

121

Then I discarded it or outgrew it.'' Those bits and pieces ranged from feathers to flower stalks to pieces of metal. Adams's genius lies in his ability to synthesize the broader strokes of the landscape with the finite detail in the plants and earth around him. His resources are the fields around his house, the junk pile by the road, and his own fertile imagination. He is a product of the desert, its coloration, aridity, and texture.

The house itself is a group of barnlike structures that have grown topsy-turvily over the years. Rooms, doors, and floors change with the passing of time, and once you have found the front door to the house, you can never be sure it will be in the same place when you return. Constantly structuring and restructuring the space has been a lifelong project for the owner, whose diminutive stature (five foot five) belies the ferocity with which he rips out ceilings and relocates stairs.

Japanese art and architecture have been a source of inspiration for Adams; nowhere is this more evident than in his use of natural woods, rich textures, and everyday objects stylized into abstract shapes. Subtle shifts in texture, coloration, and materials build the character of each room. Weathered wall-panels, the peeling-bark effect of white walls fashioned from torn Kraft paper, latticed bundles of twigs tied carefully at each juncture with tiny wires twisted into perfect little knots, suggest the subtlety and restraint of a traditional Japanese house.

Through his manipulation of an object, Adams creates something beyond the object itself. In doing this, he reveals much about style. A plow disc nestles into an Imari plate stand and suggests a rare porcelain platter. A refrigerator riddled with shotgun holes is snipped into panels and mitred to form a fireplace surround. Hatchet marks on the mantel beam attest to its previous incarnation as chopping block for the chicken house.

His representation of a Louis XVI console table is wrought from uncut corduroy dipped in paint, twisted and tied around a simple shape. He festoons the drapes and crevices with Italianate details, a bit of brocade here, a dried leaf there, and when you stand back to take it in, it feels like an eighteenth-century gilded table. No Florentine master could take issue with its humble materials. It embodies all the grace and finesse of an earlier age. After he has arranged a number of

**T**he perfect artistry with which the owner blends the elements of his surroundings is nowhere more clearly seen than in this bedroom tableau (LEFT): barn siding window louvers, table base of two-by-six scraps, basket of dried weeds, cotton duck swags cascading from the ceiling to the corners of a French country sleigh bed, Louis XV leather-covered chair, and a painted plywood floor.

**T**he rough woods and deep browns of the kitchen (BELOW) are flooded with light from the opening above. The catwalk cradles a night-blooming succulent.

**B**undled twigs clasp the base of a simple pedestal table and are joined by rustic mule-eared chairs (RIGHT). Dish storage is hidden by tansu-style sliding doors, echoes of the Oriental influence so important to Northwest design.

**T**he effect of peeling bark comes from walls papered with number three white paper, the heavy Kraft paper normally used on apple boxes, torn to reveal its brown interior, then glued to the wall (FAR TOP RIGHT).

**T**he influence of Japanese design is nowhere more apparent than in these latticed bundles of twigs tied carefully at each juncture with tiny wires twisted into perfect knots (FAR BOTTOM RIGHT).

124

Victorian mercury glass balls, buoys, and painted papier-mâché spheres on the console, flanked by faux painted wooden candlesticks, he stuffs a basket of polished antlers under the table and sets a few pieces of pottery to the side.

Then to round out the picture Adams takes a broken-looking glass, paints it with a bit of chinoiserie detail, cuts leaflike shapes from rusted metal and weathered plywood to adorn the crown, wraps the oval with string and twisted cloth, and fashions a mirror to grace the finest salon.

Creativity is often accompanied by hardship. Adams was one of twin brothers born in 1942 to an extended Yakima Indian family, primarily cattle ranchers. Amongst the Plains and Plateau Indians there existed an ancient tradition of sacrificing a weaker twin to give power and strength to the other. Long after ancient rituals pass, the mythology surrounding them lingers, and when Leo was born, legends perhaps locked into genetic memory identified him as the weaker child. He was summarily rejected by his paternal grandfather, denied his birthright of cattle, and relegated to the care of his mother.

As Adams's creativity and sensitivity flowered with age, he was shunned by a good deal of the family. At age ten he was banned from his grandfather's home permanently. "I was a weird child," says Adams, "not at all like the rest of my family, and I think that threatened them. They just didn't understand." However, he credits this isolation with fostering his creativity. Under the tutelage of his mother, he learned the crafts that fill his life today. She taught him cooking, sewing, gardening, and a reverence for the land.

After graduation from high school he spent time in Los Angeles learning fashion illustration, but the commercial art market allowed him to express none of the richness of his heritage. With tribal encouragement and some settlement funding, Adams traveled in Europe for a year to gain exposure to art and architecture. "I took pictures of surfaces and textures: walls, doors, stone, and plaster." When he returned to the Northwest, his paintings began to sell. Adams's art reflects a wide range of styles, from primitive to abstract, each stage representing a different fascination with his environment. Most recently he has concentrated on the abstract—suggestions of shapes and geometry, glowing with the tones of his surroundings, surging with the intensity of his soul.

When his artistic career began to solidify, Adams's mother encouraged him to buy some land of his own, as the Yakimas were no longer receiving land allotments at birth. He purchased acreage within a half-mile of his grandfather's house, and after his grandfather's death dragged the old homestead to his land. Ironically, he says, "I live in a house I wasn't allowed in as a child."

His fascination with the "found" object is given full expression in that house. The barn walls are often covered with natural canvas, or gray flannel blankets stretched across the wood (the quintessential neutral backdrop for his paintings).

When a friend gave Adams a large roll of number-three white (the paper commonly used on apple boxes), Adams tore the white finish to expose the inner brown reveal and papered his walls with it. His floors are sheets of plywood painted to resemble tiled or marbled surfaces. He creates the stone-work look by "washing" the floors with a rusty glaze, then gluing down squares of brown wrapping paper, texturing them with acrylic paint and sealing the whole surface with a polyurethane varnish sealer. He has plans for installing chipboard on those floors, large sheets that will be bleached and sealed. He is also planning to cover the barnlike exterior of

his house with sheets of galvanized metal, "so I don't have to paint the house in my old age." The existing silvery gray siding will be brought indoors to be used as a ceiling treatment.

Note that the living room chandelier is created from string, but has the shape and feel of its more traditional cousin. A cement-block fireplace is painted black, then chipped with hammer and chisel to give the illusion of stone. Tansu-style chests are crafted from scrap lumber and dried twigs. Most of the cushions are covered with affordable one hundred percent cotton duck, either natural or patterned with a sponge and watered-down acrylic paint.

Within this naturally crafted interior, a fine piece of Imari, one sinuously carved armoire, or an Adams painting stands out in sharp relief. The lessons are simple: no element is too humble to be mixed with a formal piece, less is more, and a copy, when done well, has all the cachet of the original, and perhaps even more.

The interweaving of land and life gives this house more than a presence. It has a flow that seems to emanate from the headwaters of the owner's Indian heritage and carry with it the flotsam and jetsam of his experience, ever moving, ever changing, but always inextricably bound to the land.

**W**eathered hickory rocking chairs sit on an aggregate patio floor. The owner's fascination with neutral colors is drawn from the subtle coloration of the Yakima Valley. He likes gray, beige, taupe, brown, cream, and white.

**T**he barnlike exterior of the house (TOP LEFT) is broken with a series of large windows designed by the owner, just as a green ribbon of fruit trees breaks the long expanse of arid ridge.

**A**dams keeps his outdoor tableaux simple and rustic, using weathered baskets and hardy white petunias (BOTTOM LEFT).

OREGON

Travelers on the interstate freeways that traverse the Northwest from the southwest tip of Wyoming to the Oregon coast, travel through three mountain ranges before they reach the fertile valleys of western Oregon. The journey can consume two days of driving time and enough energy to sorely test the modern automobile. When one considers the bravery and endurance needed to endure this journey in a covered wagon over a six month period, it staggers the imagination. The deeply rutted road cut by wagon wheels as they struggled over this hostile terrain can still be seen. Certainly the bold entrance of Captain Robert Gray into the mouth of the Columbia River in 1792 was a cakewalk by comparison.

Because of Gray's exploration of the Oregon coast and the overland trail blazed by Meriwether Lewis and William Clark in 1805, the United States had a strong claim to the land that became known as the Oregon Territory. In the 1800s this territory extended from Alaska to California, and as far east as the Rocky Mountains. A series of treaties allowed the various claimants to settle somewhat harmoniously, and fur traders started the first white settlement in what is now known as Oregon State. In 1843 the first overland migration came via the Oregon Trail to the Willamette Valley. Fed by the Willamette River and bounded by the Coastal Range and the Cascade Mountains, this valley is blessed with a temperate climate, rich soil, and navigable rivers. More than half of Oregon's population has settled in this channel of land.

With one tenth of the nation's timber blanketing Oregon's topography, early settlers found an abundance of raw material with which to build shelters. Douglas fir, spruce, and cedar were easily felled for the crude but expedient log cabins assembled as temporary houses for the first arrivals. With the aid of often hastily erected sawmills, houses of more distinct lineage began to appear. However, they were certainly not the first wooden structures built on this land. The Coastal Indians used the magnificent timbers to build permanent lodges long before white settlers began to claim the land.

The first houses built of sawn lumber borrowed heavily from East Coast and European styles. Because the raw materials were largely indigenous, exact copies of ancestral houses were difficult to achieve. Some lumber, milled and planed in the East, was shipped around the Horn. But most was milled on site from the abundant natural resources, and the houses were built by the local craftsmen. Consequently the early architecture of Oregon reflected a number of styles and building techniques adapted to suit the availability of materials and craftsmanship. Ornate dentil work, cornices, and cove moldings were often missing in early Oregon Classical Revival structures. However, as more craftsmen appeared on the frontier and techniques were refined, architectural sophistication grew.

More important to the evolution of style in Oregon was the intent with which the pioneers came to the Oregon Territory. Those settlers who left the Oregon Trail at the Dalles, where the Columbia River passes through the Cascade Mountains, and headed downriver toward the Willamette Valley, came to establish communities. They were family people, religious, often from blue chip New England families, and fairly conservative. They had come to establish agricultural communities, hence, civilization. The underpinning of their structures was stability, and their houses were built to last. They gave New England names to their towns—Portland, Salem, Medford—and were closely tied by shipping to their New England heritage. So close, in fact, that Portland very nearly became "Boston," saved only by a flip of the coin between land developers Francis Pettygrove and Asa Lovejoy (each intent on naming the newly designated port after their respective hometowns.)

Ships coming round the Horn brought architectural plan books, ideas, furniture, and clothing. As the first Greek Revival homes were being built in Pennsylvania in the 1840s, ships were bringing that knowledge to the homesteaders in Oregon where echoes of Greek Revival appear in the Willamette Valley as early as 1851. And as the pioneers got wealthier, they continued to draw on the East Coast for inspiration, carefully mapping out street lengths and grids, parks and public spaces. Pettygrove and Lovejoy platted downtown Portland street lengths in a 200- by 200-foot grid, and in 1903 the Olmsted Brothers of New York were hired to develop a park and parkway system.

In 1883 the Pacific Northern Railroad linked the Oregon Territory to the rest of the country and the Willamette Valley could be reached in four to six days. In anticipation of the linkage, financier Henry Villard invited the prestigious New York firm of McKim, Meade, and White to design railroad stations in Portland and Tacoma, Washington. Charles McKim and William Whidden of Boston arrived to inspect the sites and ultimately Whidden stayed behind to become one of the most influential forces in Portland's architectural birth. Whidden and partner Ion Lewis forever stamped Portland with the classicism of the East Coast. Whidden and Lewis were followed by luminaries such as A. E. Doyle and Pietro Belluschi, who further refined the archtypes of the East and brought national attention to this little Boston of the West.

Throughout the development of architecture in Oregon, the fundamental and very East Coast values of the pioneers gave Oregon a special kind of integrity that not only permeated the public structures, but gave Oregonians a character all their own. Imbued with a sense of transcendent values, they monitored their progress carefully, determined not to foul their own nest. When the rest of the country was heaving beer bottles out of car windows, Oregonians had forced conservation by requiring a deposit on cans and bottles. During the energy crunch of the early 1980s Oregon was the first state to institute a 55 mph speed limit and the last to lift it in 1988. The entire history of Oregon suggests a certain bravado and fearlessness tinged with responsible conservatism. Even the seemingly iconoclastic addition of the Michael Graves Portland Building to the downtown skyline, the first major public Post Modern building in the nation, reflects a basic conservatism—a daring move, yet they relied on an East Coast architect to do it for them. The charm of Oregon lies in this fundamental dichotomy. It's a place where men are not afraid to grow a beard or shoulder-length hair—as long as they're wearing a button-down collar shirt.

# State of the Art Loft

AN INDUSTRIAL

WAREHOUSE TAKES ON

NEW LIFE IN

DOWNTOWN PORTLAND

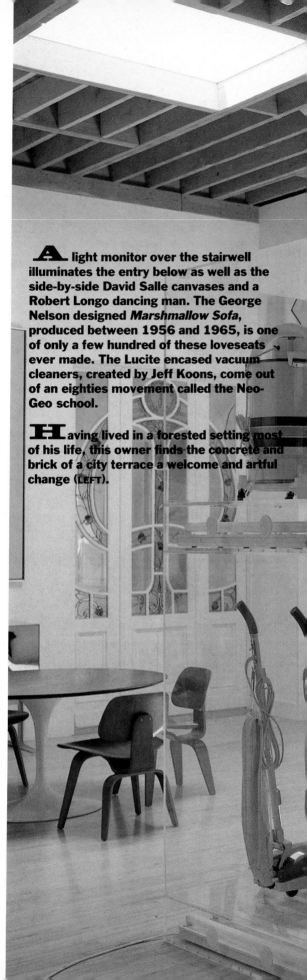

**A** light monitor over the stairwell illuminates the entry below as well as the side-by-side David Salle canvases and a Robert Longo dancing man. The George Nelson designed *Marshmallow Sofa*, produced between 1956 and 1965, is one of only a few hundred of these loveseats ever made. The Lucite encased vacuum cleaners, created by Jeff Koons, come out of an eighties movement called the Neo-Geo school.

**H**aving lived in a forested setting most of his life, this owner finds the concrete and brick of a city terrace a welcome and artful change (LEFT).

In 1986 *Architecture* magazine called Portland, Oregon, the Lazarus of American cities. Rising out of what had through neglect and oversight become an almost moribund sense of city, Portland managed to recapture much of the vision and thought that had initially gone into the planning of one of America's most liveable cities. In 1853 the city fathers gave Portland a plan unique among nascent American cities. Laying out a grid for the urban core, they divided the blocks into 200- by 200-foot squares, giving each block a compactness and visual impact unusual in urban design. The one or two buildings occupying each block had a sense of presence, and the pedestrian could not only see the buildings well, he could navigate the city with ease. The Olmsted Brothers of New York were hired to lay out a system of parks, boulevards, and long park blocks that run the length of downtown.

In spite of thoughtful planning, the post—World War II era brought with it a cavalier attitude about the rich architectural heritage, and many of the finest examples of early architecture were casualties of an exuberant "build anew" mentality. The late sixties signaled a turning point in the reckless spate of "modernization," and historic preservation became the rallying cry. In a period of twenty years Portland turned itself around, eliminating an expressway along the riverfront, adding a light rail system, preserving historic districts, providing public amenities, and resurrecting the riverfront with a broad esplanade of parkland, shops, condominiums, and restaurants.

Much of the renewal activity has centered in the downtown core and the area immediately to the south. North of the core lies the railroad station and transportation center (an award-winning design by architects Skidmore, Owings, and Merrill) and the Chinatown historic area. Close by, in what is called the Northwest Triangle, lies an area traditionally used for warehousing. The blocks are liberally peppered with antiquated low-slung warehouses, a few federal buildings, and a somewhat uncertain game plan. By zoning this area both industrial and residential, the city has paved the way for developers to offer a living experience similar to that of New York City's famed SoHo district. Numerous galleries have opened in this little SoHo of the West, and many ware-

**A** grand two-tiered stairway (TOP LEFT) leads from the street-level entry to the living area above. The long entry hall, punctuated by the original warehouse beams, houses a number of giant canvases and storage closets. All the living space is on the second floor.

**D**ramatic fifteen-foot-high walls provide ample surface for room-sized canvases (BOTTOM LEFT). Many of the skylights in the sandblasted ceiling had to be covered or eliminated to protect the collection from excessive sunlight.

**D**uane Hanson's sculpture *The Dishwasher* (ABOVE) startles with its lifelike qualities. Molded from a living person, then cast in resin, Hanson's sculptures are a mirror of the common man in the latter half of the twentieth century. The octagon on the room divider is a 1963 Frank Stella called *Henry Garden*.

This quiet corner seating area in the main gallery is flooded with morning light from the capacious eastern-facing windows. The owner found three of the four matching Knoll chairs at a garage sale a few years back. Designed by Charles Pollock, the handsome tubular steel supports carry a saddle leather sling with separate foam rubber cushion. A Don Judd stainless steel stack climbs the rear wall next to color-field artist Jules Olitski's orange canvas.

houses are being converted to artists' studios and living/working lofts.

The art collector who converted this warehouse, former location of a machine shop and then a hotel supply, had long toyed with the idea of moving his collection to a real urban setting. For twenty-five years he had lived in the forested hills outside Portland, enjoying his solitude in a Northwest contemporary home. But the lure of a New York life-style (he freely admits being a New Yorkophile) drew him searching through the industrial section of Portland for the perfect SoHo-style loft. In the late seventies he actually purchased a building, but backed out at the last minute, racked with uncertainty. He continued his love affair with New York, visiting often and buying new pieces, until his taste for the urban life and his burgeoning collection finally forced him into a place that could accommodate both his collection and his yen for city living.

"I can't believe I didn't do it ten years ago," he laments. "I don't know what took me so long." A mere eight blocks from the center of downtown, he now walks or bicycles into town or to the grocery store, rarely using his car. Friends, who had to be coaxed to his hilltop retreat with the promise of dinner and an evening's entertainment, can now simply drop by after work for a drink.

The conversion of the warehouse occurred with relative ease. He called upon his old friend Edgar Smith, who had won an architectural award for the original hilltop house, to consult with him in designing the space. Smith, who had to be coaxed out of retirement, assigned the project supervision to designer Ralph Cereghino. They planned a lower entry with garage, a long gallery, and storage area. A dramatic staircase leads to the living and entertaining areas, a two-part scheme that divides the more public space from the bedroom, kitchen, and sitting areas. Each area is heated by a separate heat pump so the owner can retire to the bedroom/kitchen area in the colder months and not sacrifice heating energy to fifteen-foot-high ceilings when the gallery area is not in use.

The actual conversion took four months, a short time, but the owner had sold his house and was moving from one set of temporary quarters to another with a mattress and TV. "I pushed like crazy," he admits. The roof is still supported by

**T**he tramp-art boxes of post—Civil War itinerants stand out against the pristine walls of this showcase space as clearly as the Charles Eames lounge chair. Stained-glass art nouveau doors, bought at auction, separate the gallery from the private section of the house where the owner can relax in more intimate surroundings.

**W**hitewashed pecan floors, once stained with engine grease, span the gallery area. The more formal dining area is defined by the positioning of a Saarinen table and classic Eames plywood chairs next to an early formed-plastic credenza designed by Raymond Loewy. A Helen Frankenthaler canvas is flanked by Andy Warhol's *Jackie*.

142

**A** ndy Warhol's soup cans, the pop art icon of the sixties, find their niche above the Eurostyled white cabinetry of this sleek and party-sized kitchen (TOP LEFT). The floor is covered with twelve-inch white marble tiles.

**C** ommercial metal shelving houses a cookie jar collection (LEFT) as whimsical yet as functional as the Eero Saarinen designed tulip chairs and pedestal table.

143

he smiles. He started collecting cookie jars long before they became popular. It all began at a flea market when he saw Clarabelle the Cow. She reminded him of his childhood. It's as simple as that.

His tramp-art collection started because the art form was foreign to him. Learning that this craft dated back to the Civil War, he became fascinated by the history of itinerant workers carving up cigar boxes and layering the pieces to make mirrors, boxes, and even furniture. "There was a time when somebody would tell me about a tramp-art piece they had seen at the beach and I'd jump in my car and drive an hour and a half to see it." Those days are gone, but his fascination with the art scene in New York continues.

"I started collecting art out of college," he remembers. "Actually I was an art student, but I was more interested in what my fellow students were painting than my own art." An initial interest in Northwest art soon gave way to serious collecting of New York artists. The first significant purchase was a 1963 geometric by Frank Stella entitled *Henry's Garden*. The latest Stella, an abstract from the Exotic Bird Series, was purchased in 1978.

Painting and sculpture of the sixties and eighties dominate his art collection. The fifties furniture collection came about quite by accident. When his first residence, the hilltop house, was built, his architect pushed for "modern" furniture to complement the architecture. Thus he found himself with Saarinen, Eames, and Knoll pieces, now extremely collectible. When a friend commented that his home looked like a furniture store, he responded by pointing out that when he has a lot of people over, no one has to stand up. There are little seating areas everywhere. "And if I run out of chairs, I have an elevator filled with them." The only problem with such a vast room is that when he invites thirty to thirty-five people, he often looks around for late arrivals only to count heads and realize they are all there.

He once thought of living in New York, but Portland offers him a life-style not really possible in the Big Apple. On a quiet summer's evening he sits on his deck, pots of annuals exploding with color, the sweep of aged brick buildings promising regeneration, and he has his piece of SoHo. "My whole life has changed," he says. "I should have done it years ago."

original old-growth timber columns topped with shear capitals. Roof joists and blocking are all exposed, giving the ceiling a corduroy pattern, a handsome textural contrast to the pristine white walls. The ceilings were sandblasted, and a few skylights were taken out to protect the paintings from harsh sunlight. The original pecan floors could not be bleached because of oil stains, so they were whitewashed and Swedish finished. An atrium was added in back to lighten the bedroom and kitchen areas, and to create a more natural transition between the living space and the deck.

The open gallery space is divided into seating areas with room dividers that double as storage closets. An inveterate collector, he is unable to display his entire art collection in the 6000-square-foot space, so many pieces are hidden in storage closets. Metal racks in the kitchen show off a good portion of his cookie jar collection, but a number of jars still languish in storage. A windup toy collection is hidden away, and a few collections, quilts and primitive art among them, were just sold off for lack of display or storage space.

Queried about his fascination with accumulating unique objects, he just shrugs his shoulders. "I like the stuff!" And

The built-in bed is covered by the lone survivor of a large quilt collection, sold off to make room for newer acquisitions. German artist Jiri Dokoupil's *IBM* forms the headpiece, while a provocative Robert Yarber night scene amuses from above the sliding glass doors that lead to the roof terrace.

Only the Saarinen chair and sculpture by artist Hilde Morris punctuate the clean lines of this bathtub retreat (LEFT), enclosed and lit by a west wall atrium addition that extends across the adjoining kitchen area.

# Historic Homestead

## A

### PIONEER FARM

### ON OREGON'S

### FRENCH PRAIRIE

**A** generous eight-foot-wide porch and peristyle of thirty-one Doric columns made this Greek Revival farmhouse (LEFT) unusually formal for its time. The red exterior paint, discovered and restored when the new owners chipped away the peeling white facade, was also atypical.

In 1859, the year construction commenced, this farmhouse was probably the largest house in Oregon. William Case, who had come to the Willamette Valley via the Oregon Trail, chose this setting on the French Prairie for its magnificent stands of timber and incredibly rich soil.

Bent willow furniture can remain under the protective eaves year round. The porch (PREVIOUS PAGE AND TOP RIGHT) is just as conducive to summer evening reflection as rainy day perambulations.

The old smokehouse, once the scene of food preserving activity, is now used as a secluded potting shed (BOTTOM RIGHT).

The undulating farmland of Oregon's Willamette Valley must have seemed like God's own garden to the weary souls who had spent six months of backbreaking, throat-wrenching effort crossing the Oregon Trail. They arrived with precious little energy, save for an indomitable will and a purpose: to bring civilization to the frontier. Their arrival usually coincided with the beginning of fall, thus hastily erected shelters, crude structures of sticks and cedar, were their only protection from the winter. But as spring inevitably broke over the valley, their spirits must have soared, fueled by a winter of recovery and a landscape of incredible promise. Here they found a gentle land, blessed with tall timbers, rushing streams, rich soil, and a temperate climate.

William Case was part of the "second wave" of settlers, arriving in the fall of 1844. He came from a prominent Indiana family that had secured an early copy of the Lewis and Clark report on the West. He followed the first homesteaders, who crossed the trail in 1843 and had staked their claims along the rivers, closer to the centers of commerce. Case had found property on the Willamette, but changed his mind in order to acquire a parcel of land in the heart of the French Prairie, a broad sweep of farmland about thirty miles south of Portland, originally settled by French fur trappers. Case's land was favored with a stream, a ravine, tall stands of old-growth timber, and easily tilled fields.

The Case Farm soon became a model of industry. Reported to be a man of indefatigable will, Case slept only five hours a night in order to construct his own sawmill, a brick kiln, blacksmith shop, a forge, smokehouse, and washhouse. While most settlers built a one-room house in anticipation of building a permanent "great house" in the ensuing five-year period, Case initially constructed a three-room log house. By 1859 he had completed the main house, a spectacular Greek Revival "temple," painted red, and reputed to be the largest farmhouse in western Oregon. Set on brick piers and borrowing heavily from the style of Southern plantation houses, the L-shaped structure was enclosed by a peristyle of thirty-one Doric columns, each cut on the property from a single Douglas fir. Generous eaves sheltered the eight-foot-wide porches, keeping the exterior walls pro-

**149**

tected from the heat and weather. A series of doors and opposing windows kept the house well ventilated, an unusual and environmentally sensitive design for the time.

Time, however, did not treat this house kindly. By 1976 the grandeur of the Case farmhouse had been largely obscured by generations of neglect and peeling paint. The outbuildings had collapsed, much of the fascia board was gone, and the house was rotting on its piers when landscape architect Wallace Huntington and interior designer Mirza Dickel decided to restore the property. Fascinated by architectural history and undaunted by the prospect of tackling this derelict Oregon landmark, they were charmed by its potential. "I was intrigued with the house because it was unrestored," Huntington says. "So much of the original fabric was there."

Fortunately the basic structure was sound. Huntington and Dickel found that peeling paint was the least compelling of defects. More pressing was the need to reroof, shore up the foundation, and replace the rotting porch. Because the house was constructed on brick piers for airflow, the foundation was accessible. The exterior walls, protected by the broad overhangs, were not only in good shape, but were so true that Huntington's carpenter could find only a one-inch variation in the entire length of the house. All of the original thirty-one columns were saved.

Each room was graced with a single light bulb hanging from an electrical cord. A water closet and sink were the only existing bathroom amenities. With the help of architect Charles Gilman Davis, Huntington and Dickel set about

**D**ishes and dry goods were once stored in cupboards over the fireplace which now hold reference books. Oregon pine worktables and wing chairs flank the fireplace, and an English Regency chair sits in the foreground.

**W**ith six exterior doors opening into the living and dining areas, the main entry is difficult to discern (FAR LEFT). This door leads into the former dining room, now a sitting area flanked by an antique American tiger-maple chest and a charming collection of silhouettes.

**T**his doorway (LEFT) joins what was once the men's sitting room and the dining room. The original dining room cupboards (at rear) now house an old book collection. A seventeenth-century English mulberry chest and eighteenth-century English chinoiserie clock flank the doorway.

The wide dining room table (FAR LEFT) is a walnut burl surrounded by late-eighteenth-century George III chairs covered with the original petit point. An upholsterer had to work from underneath in order to restore the seats. The stairs at rear lead to a large attic that probably housed field workers at harvest time.

The tall Oregon pine cupboard (LEFT), found in recent years in Olympia, Washington, has a flip knob like all the doors and cupboards in the house. The blue and white pottery came from China often via England. The better pieces, called Chinese Export, were originally commissioned, and others, known as Canton, were used as ballast on ships to England.

to effectively convert one of the six seven- by ten-foot bedrooms, lined three by three down a long hall, to a bathroom. Two others became dressing rooms for the closetless bedroom wing.

Davis designed the cabinetry for the kitchen, which had a long journey into the late-twentieth century. While dishwashers and garbage disposers were not exactly "period" pieces, neither Huntington nor Dickel wanted to replicate the life-style of the 1800s. Thus they created a modern kitchen using the vernacular of the old farmhouse: wooden countertops, a wood stove, and cabinetry milled to match existing cupboards. Their aesthetic concessions included hiding the refrigerator in a pass-through alcove and eliminating a grease screen behind the range.

Scrapings of exterior paint revealed that the farmhouse had originally been painted red, an unusual color for Greek Revival houses. The interior walls were generally single planks of vertical wood from floor to ceiling. This was a typical late-nineteenth-century method of construction employing less lumber and allowing greater speed. The only real construction anomaly is the vaulted wooden ceiling in the bedroom wing; there was no structural reason for a barreled ceiling. It seemed to be purely an aesthetic touch, as was the large glass door at the end of the hall.

Evidently William Case was a man of great aesthetic sensibility, for the house reflects genuine concern with detail. Aside from the vaulted ceiling, the proportions of the rooms are quite grand. A ceiling height of nine feet six inches gives

The owners have picked up whimsical wire kitchen implements in junk shops around the area. Most of the pieces are handmade (RIGHT).

Neither the wood stove nor the large view window is original to the kitchen (FAR RIGHT), but the warmth of the room transcends any concessions to twentieth-century living. The present owners, like their predecessors, use the stove for slow soups and stews. The blue rawhide-seated side chairs are early Oregon pieces.

the rooms ample height, and the overall proportions of the house, nearly ninety by one hundred feet, make it highly ambitious for an Oregon farmhouse. An eighteen-inch skirt-board rises from the hard old-growth fir floors, and the line carries across doors milled to match the skirt. The windows are long, six-over-six, thin muntinned, and double-hung.

The woodshed, at thirty-eight by thirty-eight feet, is larger than many farmhouses. Although no records exist to indicate why Case built a woodshed of such immense proportions, a similar farmhouse in Gervais has a record of using 400 cords of wood one winter. The Case house had a wood stove, three fireplaces, and a washhouse with a water heater to fire.

The French Prairie is still peopled with the descendants of William Case, and part of the charm of restoring the house

has been the revelation of history that has come with it. Huntington and Dickel have pored through historical records to learn more about the farm and its owners, yet some of the most fascinating information has come through neighbors and friends. "The historical records won't tell you," Huntington says, "that Mrs. Case brought with her a black slave." Nor will they tell you that William Case was not a very likeable man. He was notorious for driving his help and the animals. The Cases had thirteen children, but only two sons. Remarkably, most of the girls were educated at Willamette University, but when one of the boys went off to fight in the Indian wars, Case disowned him.

Huntington is quick to add, "He must have cared about things." Not only did he create a house of gracious propor-

tion and unusual sensitivity to detail, he also furnished the farmhouse with well-crafted pieces. "He had good furniture, made out of maple, not just thrown together of fir." His bed, based on an eighteenth-century prototype, was specially designed for his towering stature. While most antique beds have to be restructured for modern use, these honey-colored four-posters, at six feet six inches, are big enough to sleep in today.

Happily, much of the Case furniture found its way back to the farmhouse once Huntington and Dickel had finished the restoration. Northwest historian Burt Brown Barker had collected a number of early Oregon pieces, and when he died, his daughter carried on his interest, supplying the farmhouse and the local historical museum. The rest of the furniture, a fine collection of English and American antiques, represents a lifetime of collecting for the owners. "When we started," Dickel remembers, "we had a number of French and Italian pieces, which we sold or traded."

Huntington had lived in a large Portland Victorian, a gorgeous house on the National Register of Historic Places, but poorly sited for an avid gardener. He saw the farmhouse

as an idyllic garden site with a wonderful sense of enclosure and a clear view of Mount Hood, Oregon's reigning queen of vistas. When the restoration was complete, he set about to formalize the gardens with a combination of shrubs and perennials. Sated by client requests for evergreens, rhododendrons, and azaleas, his own garden reflects an English influence. Prize magnolia specimens, fine old roses, and deciduous trees such as lilac, viburnum, weigela, and witch hazel are reminiscent of older garden styles. The cutting garden overflowed with cosmos, baby's breath, salpaglossis, sweet pea, delphinium, daisies, euphorbia, peonies, and nicotiana, which spill into the house in the form of Mirza Dickel's loose and eclectic bouquets.

Whether enjoying a soft summer breeze blowing through the open doors or lingering by the fire on a winter's eve, the owners feel a continuity of life-style. After reminiscing about the transformation of this crumbling derelict and the changes that have occurred, Huntington says, "They must have been great conversationalists. When we entertain, we think of the overnight guests who must have lingered by the fire, talking long into the evening. Some things never change."

▲ ▲ ▲ ▲ ▲ ▲ ▲ ▲ ▲ ▲ ▲   ▲

**T**he unusually spacious attic (FAR LEFT), once housing for field workers, now stores part of the owners' Oregon pottery collection. In 1865 the Smith family from Iowa started the Oregon Pottery Company and supplied the settlers with clay vessels for storing, preserving, and preparing food.

**S**ix seven-by-ten bedrooms open onto this barrel-vaulted hallway (MIDDLE LEFT). The owners have converted one to a bath, and two to dressing rooms in this closetless wing. The small desk, made of Oregon saplings, has a pull-out shelf to expand the work area.

**T**his unusually generously proportioned bed (LEFT) measures six feet three inches on the inside and was commissioned by the original owner, William Case. The bedspread is hand-woven double-weave cotton from the 1850s. The present owners researched stenciling patterns for the locally made shades.

157

# Coastal Classic

## RUSTIC SIMPLICITY

## ON THE

## GRASSY DUNES

## OF GEARHART

**W**alls of variegated local stone and clear cedar provide a natural background for the owners' collection of Asian and Southwest-influenced furnishings. The birch daybeds and Parsons dining table are original to the house. The cactus arrangements were created by the owners.

**T**he Pacific once lay just beyond the back door (LEFT). But half a century of accumulated sand has rendered the ocean nearly invisible, prompting the current owners to contemplate adding a second story addition.

▲ ▲ ▲ ▲ ▲ ▲ ▲ ▲ ▲ ▲ ▲ ▲ ▲ ▲ ▲ ▲ ▲ ▲ ▲ ▲ ▲ ▲ ▲ ▲ ▲ ▲ ▲

**I**ts low profile and natural materials help blend the house designed by Pietro Belluschi with its seaside setting (ABOVE). Beach grass planted during the Depression anchored the shifting dunes but allowed drifting sand to accumulate, causing the shoreline to recede.

**T**he 1943 house exemplified the emerging Northwest Contemporary Style. Wide, sheltering eaves, indigenous board-and-batten siding, native stone, and large, view-embracing windows broke down divisions between interior and exterior, creating a house in perfect harmony with its surroundings (TOP).

**C**lear cedar lines the walls and ceiling of the entry foyer (RIGHT), which is furnished with stripped hickory chairs and its own fireplace. The painting above it is by Northwest artist Louis Bunce. The house features poured concrete floors in the manner of Frank Lloyd Wright, who had been an acquaintance of the architect.

**U**nlike Washington's rugged and often inhospitable coast, the Oregon shore is smooth, sandy, and accessible. Never more than ninety minutes away from the principal cities in western Oregon, the beach beckons weekend vagabonds primed for miles of fine sand and salty spray.

One of the coast's most fashionable retreats is Gearhart, located seventy-five miles northwest of Portland near the mouth of the Columbia. This city of 1,100 year-round residents has thankfully avoided the kite shops and croissanteries that frequently overrun other seashore communities. The folks in Gearhart have paid a premium for their privacy, but the result is a bewitching blend of natural splendor and creature comfort.

The history of the city dates back to 1848, when Philip Gearhart, an Iowa farmer, settled his family on 600 acres just north of the Necanicum River. It wasn't until 1898, when the railroad connecting Portland and neighboring Seaside was completed, that vacation cottages started springing up.

Even then, it took a good five hours to travel from Portland to Gearhart. Families would pile onto the train the day after school let out and not return to the city until the waning days of summer. On Friday afternoons, fathers boarded the "Daddy Train" to join their families for the weekend.

The homes built in Gearhart in the last years of the nineteenth century were usually modest versions of Queen Anne and Stick Style city houses. By the teens and twenties, bungalows and simplified colonials were the style of choice. It wasn't until Portland architect A. E. Doyle designed a series of beach houses in Neahkahnie around 1915 that an indigenous style began to emerge. Doyle's simple, woodsy cottages, which featured wide, overhanging eaves and large, vertically divided windows, would eventually serve as the inspiration for the Northwest Style popularized by Portland architect Pietro Belluschi.

Belluschi was born in 1899 in a small town near Venice, Italy. He emigrated to the U.S. in 1923 to attend graduate school at Cornell University. Settling in Portland, he got a job in A. E. Doyle's office and soon advanced to chief designer. The architect first achieved national recognition with his design for the Portland Art Museum, completed in 1932. His

**N**ineteenth-century bamboo chairs from China flank a lacquer table covered with Japanese Sumida Gawa ware in the bedroom hallway (LEFT).

**T**he contemporary but timeless design of the house is the perfect setting for a collection of baskets, Asian antiques, and contemporary art. A 100-year-old Indian basket adorns the center of the dining room table, while the built-in buffet is home to an assortment of ceramic pieces and a pair of nineteenth-century folding Japanese candlesticks. The paintings by Fay Jones (left) and Joe Baker flank hanging baskets from the Philippines (FAR LEFT).

efforts to establish a regional approach to design were realized in his own home, built in Portland in 1936. The natural spruce siding and the hipped and gable roof forms gave the house a rural quality heretofore unseen in the city.

Seven years later Belluschi designed what many—including the architect—consider one of his finest residences. The Kerr house was built for Peter Kerr, an eighty-year-old Scotsman who made his fortune in the grain export business. Erected on a then-deserted stretch of grass at the north end of Gearhart, the 4,500-square-foot house features a low-pitched gable roof that mimics the contour of the site,

uniting structure and setting while providing a sense of shelter against the harsh coastal climate. The use of naturally weathered board-and-batten siding is reminiscent of the vernacular barns of Oregon, while the siding's narrow channels seem to mimic the slender blades of beach grass that nuzzle the exterior. The lone log column supporting the entry porch was discovered on the beach and added to the design as a kind of author's homage to his source material.

Floor-to-ceiling windows in the living room break down formal barriers between interior and exterior, blending the two in a manner evocative of traditional Japanese design.

**T**he master bedroom looks out over a field of waving beach grass and a shimmering band of ocean. At the foot of the bamboo four-poster, a tansu top serves as a table. The unusual chest on the far wall is made of keyaki wood and is adorned with etched iron hardware.

The extended eaves seem to embrace the view while sheltering the interior from severe winter storms. The light passing underneath is shadowy and cool—the kind of light that inspires tranquillity and contemplation.

The present owners have been coming to the area every summer since they were children. The husband, a cardiologist, vacationed in Seaside as a youth, while the wife, the executive vice president of a medical electronics company, frolicked at the venerable Gearhart Hotel, a 100-room, shingle-style resort that was demolished back in 1972.

The couple already owned a house in Gearhart when the third owners of the Kerr house called to say they were selling. Still, the couple was so smitten with the house, they made an offer that day. "There wasn't a way in the world we could not buy this house," says the wife. "We were totally taken by it." They've kept the other house in the family, but consider the Kerr house their primary retreat.

Although overshadowed today by some of its more ostentatious neighbors, the house still possesses a serenity and stability that mark it as a classic. "The minute you open the door you feel like you're in another world," says the wife. "It's very restful."

**J**apanese dolls
adorn a 150-year-
old tansu chest in
the master
bedroom.
Note the ornate
ironwork adorning
the chest.

165

While storms can hit the house with ferocious intensity, the interior very rarely feels gloomy. "Even though it's cloudy a lot, you don't even see the clouds. You just see the light," attests the wife. Belluschi backed up this natural illumination with a system of cove lights ringing each room. Rows of incandescent bulbs bounce diffuse illumination off the ceiling, preventing glare from reflecting off the view-framing windows.

The interior echoes the exterior's rustic simplicity. A rugged wall made of variegated local stone forms the physical and spiritual soul of the house. The wall frames back-to-back fireplaces in both the living room and entry foyer. A marble pre-Columbian mask from Mr. Kerr's collection was embedded in the wall over the living room fireplace as a whimsical accent. Stone pillars anchor the corners of the room, lending a cavelike sense of solidity and calm.

The interior walls are covered in clear cedar, laid horizontally and left to age to a warm golden orange. The floors throughout the public spaces are poured concrete, much in the manner of Frank Lloyd Wright, who was an acquaintance

of the architect's. Stretches of natural cocoa matting lend warmth underfoot and help define living spaces within the lofty public rooms.

Belluschi's original furnishings for the home have been carefully preserved by the past owners. The pieces echo the house's simple lines and horizontal design. The living room features a pair of blond birch daybeds designed to double as extra sleeping space for visiting guests. A set of matching armchairs with deep, slunk-back seats frame a parsons table in the same pale wood. Roosevelt-era blinds made with hefty

**A**n English pine table from about 1850 (LEFT) separates the living room and dining room. Grouping the Chinese porcelain and square baskets creates a visual effect much stronger than if the pieces stood on their own.

**A**n artful arrangement of Asian accessories top the coffee table in the master bedroom (ABOVE).

167

**A** 150-year-old picture frame fitted with a mirror hangs above a nineteenth-century chest in the hallway of what was once the maid's quarters (RIGHT).

**S**quashy feather beds and Persian print duvets help ward off the sea's damp chill. The wicker chair is from Africa (FAR RIGHT).

slats of satiny birch are a nostalgic throwback to the days before window coverings went mini.

Upholstered pieces have been covered with a Southwest-inspired print in rust and white. The desert motif is a natural match for the rugged stone fireplace, natural wood walls, and oversized rooms. The effect is heightened by the cactus arrangements covering every tabletop. The present owners create the arrangements during their weekend retreats, grouping unusual varieties of cactus in old Chinese porcelain planters. "Flowers just don't work in this house," admits the wife, who collects art, deals in antiques, and practices interior design in addition to her business pursuits.

The massive fireplace is balanced by a hefty concrete coffee table by Los Angeles designer C. R. Machado. Nearly six feet across, it took seven men (recruited at curbside and in the neighborhood grocery) to carry the 400-pound disk into the house.

Stripped hickory chairs are used in both the entry foyer and dining room as a natural accompaniment to the home's rustic splendor. These pieces are complemented by a sub-

stantial collection of Northwest contemporary art, as well as Asian furnishings and accessories that the wife has accumulated on her travels throughout the world.

Nearly every room features its own tansu chest, the rarest a 150-year-old piece made from keyaki wood and adorned with etched iron hardware. Sumi drawings hang in the guest bedrooms, while the hallway outside is host to a colorful assortment of Sumida Gawa ware—a whimsical line of Japanese ceramics manufactured just prior to World War II and sometimes referred to as "Poo" ware.

The wife is passionate about baskets and features clusters of them throughout the interior. While some are contemporary, most are antiques, dating back more than sixty years. "They're very functional," she says, pointing to a flat, square basket on the dining room wall. "They hold just about anything you want to put in them. I think they're beautiful on a table, and I like what happens to them as you use them." Indeed, the basket's chestnut-brown interior has worn to a satiny smoothness with time.

The home is a magnet for the couple's five grown children and their families, who often drop in for a bowl of bouillabaisse (a specialty of the house) or a steaming pot of clams gathered fresh from the beach. In summer, dinner is preceded by cocktails on the deck, accompanied by the dull roar of the surf and the cry of the gulls overhead. In the distance, Tillamook Head maintains its vigil over the coast, disappearing from time to time in a foggy white shroud.

When the house was first built, the Pacific lay just beyond the back door. Today, only a sliver is visible on the horizon. Beach grass, planted by the U.S. Soil Conservation Service during the Depression, stabilized the dunes but allowed blowing sand to accumulate, prompting a buildup that has caused the shoreline to recede considerably.

The owners plan to build an addition that will recapture some of the ocean view lost to the sands of time. The extension will include a second-story master suite and an expanded dining room and kitchen.

The couple had just one architect in mind for the job. And so it happens that, nearly half a century after designing the original home, Pietro Belluschi is returning to the grassy dunes of Gearhart. "It was important that he do it," stresses the wife, "so that the house would maintain its character."

IDAHO

A magnificent collage of rivers, canyons, mountains, lakes, and painted deserts, Idaho lays claim to some of the Northwest's most varied and scenic countryside. From the cascading falls of the Snake River to the golden glow of sunset over the Grand Tetons, the Gem State is packed with picture-book beauty and a quiet sense of reserve shared by its people.

Sparsely populated and spiritually diverse, Idaho is a complex state that defies easy categorization. Its exotic, often inaccessible terrain (forty percent of the state is forest) creates internal divisions that are heightened by strong outside influence from the seven states and one province that share its borders.

The state can be divided into three regions. The northern panhandle is a gentle wilderness wedged between Washington and Montana. Physically removed from the rest of the state, the people who live in the panhandle consider Spokane, Washington, their regional center. The dry southeast part of the state was settled by Mormons moving north from Utah. Not surprisingly, this area looks to nearby Salt Lake

City (home of the Mormon church) for its spiritual, economic, and political inspiration. The southwest corner of the state is dominated by Boise, Idaho's capital. This city of 100,000 exerts a strong influence on its region, often to the exclusion of the rest of the state.

Over sixty percent of Idaho's land is owned by the federal government. It's not surprising, then, that more than half of its citizens live in urban areas—many in the cities clustered around the Snake River. That waterway cuts a 1,000-mile swath from Yellowstone National Park, across southern Idaho, and up along the state's western border. The Snake River's deep, narrow gorge is dotted with magnificent waterfalls and humming hydroelectric plants, while its shores are home to fertile farmland carved from what was once desolate terrain.

Idaho's climate is relatively moderate, owing to the warm breezes that blow in from the Pacific and to the high mountains to the east that block the cold blasts from Canada and the Great Plains. The state's natural resources provide Idaho with its chief sources of income, which range from agricultural products (like the legendary Idaho potato) to minerals (the state leads the nation in silver production) to timber.

The state's allure has not been lost on vacationers, who flock to Idaho in ever-increasing numbers to take in skiing, fishing, and hiking. The most famous attraction is Sun Valley. This playground of the rich was developed in 1936 by the Union Pacific Railroad and its chairman of the board, Averell Harriman, who hoped to bolster business by creating a destination for tourism. Thanks to the steady stream of celebrities coursing its slopes, Sun Valley almost singlehandedly popularized the sport of skiing in this country. The resort continues to attract crowds with its appealing combination of sunshine, slopes, and snow.

While Idahoans are justly proud of their mountain ranges, rivers, streams, and lakes, the population is divided as to whether they should conserve the state's natural resources or develop them to foster economic growth.

The specter of development has reared its head since the early days of the nineteenth century, when Lewis and Clark became the first white men to set foot on Idaho soil. In the decades that followed, Spain, Russia, Great Britain, and the U.S. all laid claim to parts of the area, as trappers competed fiercely for the region's furs.

But it was gold, not furs, that first attracted widespread attention to the state. In 1860 gold was discovered in the panhandle on Orofino Creek. Two years later, more was found down south in the Boise Basin. Soon, the area was flooded with gold seekers as towns sprouted up from the wilderness almost overnight.

The gold rush exacerbated relations with the Indians, who watched as prospectors overran their reservations and settlers appropriated their land. Although the federal government drafted treaties with the Indians, they were seldom kept. Finally, in 1877, the Nez Percé turned on the settlers. The following year the Bannock Indians rebelled. In 1879 the Sheepeaters followed suit. In all three instances, the tribes were defeated and forced to give up their land, marking the end of major Indian wars in Idaho.

The region remained a territorial ward of the federal government until 1890, when Idaho was named the forty-third state. (The name "Idaho" had originally been selected for Colorado, but was rejected because it was not an Indian word.) Statehood may have given the citizens an identity, but it did nothing for the built environment, which continued to take its cue from outside sources. House plans drafted in Chicago and New York were published daily in *The Idaho Statesman*, while others could be purchased at the local lumberyard or contractor's office for as little as eight dollars. Mass-pro-duced building components and ornaments were sold through catalogs, insuring that a house in Twin Falls could look just like a house in Niagara Falls.

By the 1920s wealthy Idahoans were visiting California regularly and asking builders back home to replicate the Mission-style houses they admired there. At least these were more appropriate to the desert climate than the colonial, English half-timbered and bungalow styles that populated Idaho's streets at the time. Although a few regional consistencies emerged, like a propensity for using native stone, Idaho never established an indigenous architectural style.

Today few Idahoans have the resources to commission custom-designed homes. The noteworthy work that does exist is usually created by outsiders either moving to the state or building a second home there—many in the area around Sun Valley.

Diverse though they may be, each of the houses pictured here celebrates the spirit of the natural world around it. Whether they're traditional log construction or state-of-the-art solar, the houses acknowledge the materials, weather, climate, and scenery of their surroundings. For it is man's relationship to the environment that built Idaho, and man's relationship to the environment that will dictate its future.

# Lakeside Artistry

## SWEDISH CHARM

## IN AN

## IDAHO COTTAGE

**A**utumn color surrounds the hillside house, which is situated on fifty-five acres abutting Black Lake in northern Idaho.

**G**olden light radiates from the house at twilight (LEFT). The front porch's willowy archway and decorative spindles were modeled after 18th-century Scandinavian farmhouse designs.

**G**eorge Carlson is a sculptor and painter whose stunning depictions of primitive life have earned him a place in many of the nation's top museums and collections.

For nearly two decades, the artist has focused his attention on the Tarahumara Indians of northern Mexico. In rough-hewn bronzes and vivid pastels, Carlson captures the beauty and nobility of a people at one with nature and oblivious to the ways of twentieth-century man.

Carlson has chosen a similar path in his own life. After years of shuffling back and forth between houses in Colorado and the Bay Area, the artist set down roots on a fifty-five-acre estate in northern Idaho. There, among the sylvan hills and placid lakes, he and wife Pamela have established a closer bond with nature and with their own ethnic heritage.

The couple's Swedish-style home rests at the foot of a hill twenty-two miles from St. Maries, Idaho. Aspens and weeping birches line the driveway to the red and white cottage, where time and tensions fade as quickly as an autumn frost. Inside, hearty pine floorboards, timeworn antiques, and cheerfully painted wainscoting capture the stalwart beauty of Sweden's indigenous design, while gracefully proportioned windows frame the reflection of stately Idaho hills in the mirror stillness of neighboring Black Lake.

For the owners, both of whom are half-Swedish, the home was a labor of love and a nostalgic return to their ancestral origins. Says George Carlson, ''I suppose a lot of people are going back to their roots, and that's pretty much what this was about—tying in to things that were familiar to our own ethnic background.''

For the Chicago-born artist, the inspiration was a cabin his family owned in Skansen, a Scandinavian enclave in rural Wisconsin. There, vacations were forged with memories of dances that lasted until four A.M., followed by hearty *sill* (fish) breakfasts of smoked herring, potatoes, hardtack, and lingonberries.

Childhood memories shaped the spirit of the new home, while books provided the architectural detailing.

''We did a tremendous amount of research on Scandinavian houses,'' the owner says. ''In fact, we took in primarily Norway and Sweden and a little bit of influence out of Fin-

A statue of St. Francis watches over a spring behind the house. The figure's enclosure came from a Colorado monastery.

**L**og beams lend rustic charm to the living room, which features a hanging light fixture designed by turn-of-the-century Spokane architect Kirtland Cutter. The shelf over the window displays some of the duck decoys the owner has collected over the last thirty years.

180

land. But when you get right down to it, it's definitely a Swedish house. It just has that feeling."

Initially, the Carlsons were just going to spend their summers there. But the lure of the Idaho retreat was so great that after three years they decided to sell the Colorado and California houses and live there full-time.

The cozy, 1,900-square-foot cottage boasts traditional board-and-batten siding, long favored by Scandinavians for its ability to shed water and expand and contract with the weather. George modeled the sculptured battens after those found in his family's Wisconsin retreat. Red siding is popular in Sweden, where native clay pigments produce a durable stain that lasts for decades. Finials grace the gable ends; their abstract designs inspired by traditional symbols used to ward off evil spirits. The custom dates back to the Vikings, who always had a dragon on top of their houses for protection. After the Vikings were Christianized, the designs became more abstract, so as not to arouse suspicion from visiting missionaries.

The protruding front porch is based on Scandinavian country farmhouse designs of the 1700s. The willowy arch-

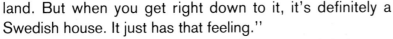

**T**he 300-year-old Dutch kas (far right) stands alongside a George Carlson sculpture in the living room. The doorway to the front hall and stairway to the second floor are visible through the arch, which is topped by a cluster of Tibetan vessels, Swedish candlesticks, and an old yoke (ABOVE LEFT).

**T**he living room's lofty ceilings were designed to accommodate the kas (ABOVE RIGHT), which was made in Holland around 1680. The coffee table was originally used by Basque shepherds, who placed coals in the center for cooking. The sculpture at right is by Leonard Baskin.

**181**

**A** French pearwood dining table (RIGHT), scarred by generations of use, sits beneath a chandelier from the Wisconsin cottage where the owner spent his childhood summers. A bird feeder lining the windowsill provides diners with a mealtime diversion.

**T**he nineteenth-century Mennonite corner cupboard (BELOW) is topped with a stuffed hen—a wedding gift from a friend. The dining room's bright walls are a traditional Swedish cure for long, dark winters.

**T**his sixty-year-old loom (FAR TOP RIGHT) fills one wall of the dining room, pending construction of a weaving studio. To the left sits an Amish ladder; to the right, a seventeenth-century old woman's suitcase from Sweden. The kilim rug is from Afghanistan.

**A** breadbox has been converted into a spice cabinet in the kitchen (FAR BOTTOM RIGHT). The countertops are vertical-grain coast fir.

way is flanked by rows of gracefully carved spindles framing a weathered pine door. The entry leads to a mudroom replete with built-in cupboards and shelves filled with decorative paraphernalia: an African gourd bowl, an old Swedish box, a contemporary ceramic vase, and a pair of primitive dolls. Coat hooks line the purple and teal trimmed hallway leading past the kitchen, where Pamela Carlson, a designer of wearable art, serves up generous helpings of wholesome Scandinavian cuisine.

"We both wanted the kitchen to have a nice, airy feeling," explains the owner, who decided to forgo upper cabinets in favor of a pair of ventilated pantries modeled after those found in the American Southwest. Air enters through a grill at the bottom of the pantries and exits out a passage at the top, keeping the contents cool year-round. White painted beadboard covers the kitchen's walls and ceiling, proffering a cozy counterpoint to the pine cupboards and solid fir countertops. An old breadbox is born again as a spice cupboard, while across the room an antique home-economics table is home to an Amish candleholder and bowls brimming over with fresh fruit.

Here, as elsewhere, the floors are made from tamarack (also known as Alpine larch), a variety of deciduous conifer noted for its brilliant autumnal color. The Carlsons purchased a truckload of tamarack logs and had them custom-milled, dried, and planed for use in the house. While further drying has led to gaps between the floorboards, the result only adds to the home's authentic charm.

The dining room is a cheerful throwback to Swedish peasant houses, where bright colors compensate for long, dark winters. Outfitted in vibrant shades of orange, green, and blue to represent the earth, the trees, and the sky, the juxtaposition recalls George Carlson's kaleidoscopic pastels.

Pamela Carlson's four-harness loom sits squarely against one wall, awaiting construction of a new studio where the designer can resume production of her one-of-a-kind garments. A French pearwood dining table hugs the far wall, illuminated by a row of tall, narrow windows draped with a piece of Battenburg lace. At mealtime, diners may gaze out at bluejays and Oregon juncos feasting from the feeder lining the windowsill.

The plate rail circling the room is host to a plethora of

**183**

The rustic front door opens onto a mudroom lined with cupboards (ABOVE).

Painted beadboard walls are paired with tamarack floors and cabinets in the country-style kitchen (ABOVE RIGHT). Vented pantries take the place of upper cabinets, adding to the room's lightness. A classroom home-economics table from the late-nineteenth century comes equipped with its own swing-out stools.

The hutch in the dining room (FAR RIGHT) once belonged to circus showman P. T. Barnum. The knotty pine ceiling recalls Swedish peasant houses, as do the vivid wall colors, which symbolize earth (orange), trees (green), sky (blue), and thistle (violet).

antiques and memorabilia collected on the couple's frequent travels. "I'm a pack rat," says the owner, who has been collecting antiques since he was seventeen. "I carry things around for years. A lot of stuff ends up in boxes, and then eventually you find just the right place for it."

Every piece has its own story, which the owners share with obvious relish. The hutch, they note, originally came from P. T. Barnum's home in Denver. The decorative moldings were used in the restoration of Molly Brown's house. The 300-year-old *kas* (cupboard) in the living room came from Holland. Its owners shipped it to America in the 1930s, fearing the rise of the Nazis. In fact, a restorer found a faded clipping about Adolf Hitler in one of the drawers.

The sofa and matching chairs once belonged to an early owner of the property, a madam who maintained a brothel in Butte, Montana. "She used to swim across this lake with her dog every day until she was eighty," notes George Carlson.

A filigreed balustrade, modeled after one found in a book, frames the sturdy fir treads leading to the second floor landing. There, a tiny window overlooks the living room below. The window was modeled after one in the house of Carl

Larsson, the Swedish artist whose country house has served as an archetype for generations of Europeans.

The Spartan master bedroom features a New England rope bed (named for the rope supports under the mattress) topped with crisp Swedish linens. A French-Canadian wardrobe from around 1800 augments the home's minimal closet space—one of the few drawbacks of living full-time in a summer home.

Across the hall, a pristine white bathroom contrasts horizontal wainscoting and vertical beadboard walls with scrubbed pine floors and a freestanding clawfoot tub. The period pedestal sink is topped with a cake of natural white soap, while fluffy terry towels hang from an old pine rack.

In the winter, Pamela fills the house with pine boughs, baby's breath, and holly for the annual observance of St. Lucia's Day, December thirteenth. As family members gather around the dining room table, the smell of *gravlox* (marinated salmon), Swedish meatballs, ham, red cabbage, lingonberries, and Swedish pastry permeates the air.

Come June the festivities move outdoors. The house is hung with birch leaves and a sumptuous smorgasbord is served on the lawn to commemorate Midsummer's Eve, the start of summer in Sweden.

In warm weather, the couple often takes lunch in the backyard grotto, a stone-lined terrace covered with a cooling white arbor. An English-style garden soon overtakes the front lawn, as bees buzz among exuberant clusters of cosmos, delphiniums, foxgloves, lilies, daisies, bluebells, and assorted herbs, while spirea runs rampant along the adjoining hillside.

The Carlsons' property extends from Black Lake to the crest of the hill behind the house. From the summit, morning mist shrouds the valley like a blanket, slowly burning off to reveal the striped fields and spring-fed lakes that lie in a chain below.

It's a twenty-minute motorboat ride from their dock to George Carlson's sculpture studio, a former church and Masonic Temple where the artist fashions the twelve-foot-high monuments that grace museums, corporate buildings, and university campuses throughout the nation. Across the driveway from the main house stands his painting and drawing studio. Designed much like the house, the one-room

The master bedroom is a testament to Swedish simplicity, although its components are international: a New England rope bed, Mexican armchair, and French peasant basket.

A Chippendale mirror hangs above the old pine chest in the children's bedroom (FAR LEFT). George Carlson's sculpture illustrates an Indian folk tale. The ivory spoon was made by a member of the Tlingit tribe, while the belts were woven by the Tarahumara Indians of Mexico.

Everything in the master bath (MIDDLE LEFT) is a crisp, clean white, save for the hearty tamarack floors and old English towel rack.

The warped door and gaps in the wainscoting and floor only add to the master bath's old-world charm (LEFT).

structure is illuminated by a large overhead window. A ledge lined with animal skulls overlooks a sturdy wooden easel and a table strewn with more than a thousand sticks of pastel.

Just up the hill sits a playhouse that was fashioned for George Carlson's daughter. Daisies grow in the window box and a scalloped ridge beam decorates the roof. A plaque over the front door bears the inscription *Andra's Nisse Hus*—Andra's Gnome House.

The Carlsons were somewhat less successful in naming the main house. After scanning a Swedish dictionary, the pair settled on *Brännvin*, or "Water of Life," as an appropriate appellation for their lakeside retreat. It wasn't until later, when they mentioned the name to a Swedish sculptor friend, that the couple learned that *Brännvin* is a popular name for aquavit—a Scandinavian liquor. The "water of life" turned out to be firewater!

**G**eorge Carlson works with more than a thousand different colors of pastel.

**B**irdhouses dot the property. This one stands guard over the painting and drawing studio, located just across the driveway from the main house (LEFT).

**G**eorge Carlson creates his vivid pastels in this well ordered studio (RIGHT). Old animal skulls overlook shelves bursting with art books, while a microscope and nature study supplies provide an occasional diversion from the easel.

# Wright Legacy

**P**erched on a knoll above the Snake River Canyon, the house was originally the studio of Archie Teater, a landscape painter. When Henry Whiting purchased the house, Teater's drop cloth was still on the floor.

**F**ollowing the owner's design, Kent Hale, the original stonemason, constructed the rock walls that lead down to the Cadenza, a detached studio hanging over the canyon walls (LEFT).

The Snake River makes a dramatic white water turn near the town of Bliss, Idaho, as it wends its way toward the Columbia. This small section of rapids is the only remaining southern Idaho portion of the river to exhibit some of its former ferocity. The heavily dammed Snake is now host to a number of slack water pools and simmering confrontation between power brokers and environmentalists. Perched on a promontory above that curve sits the sole house in Idaho designed by Frank Lloyd Wright. Appropriately, people who raft the river below refer to the white water as the Frank Lloyd Wright rapids. He would have been proud!

Southern Idaho is a vast stretch of scrub brush and dust, saved only by the mighty Snake, which nourishes and beautifies this desolate portion of the Northwest. It was largely ignored by the Oregon Trail settlers groping their way over its convoluted and inhospitable terrain. However, David and Lydia Bliss, who had grown weary of the rising population in Denver and Boise, brought their three children to the Snake River plains in 1878 and gave their name to the small settlement of Bliss. Today, with a population just over 200, the town of Bliss is better known as the western gateway to the Hagerman Valley, a vast aquifer and sportsman's paradise.

Thousands of years before man put his mark upon the land, volcanic activity repeatedly spread lava over the Snake River Plain, gradually forcing the river southward, and covering the riverbed with spongy layers of basalt. Water trapped below the surface formed its own system of reservoirs and conduits as it continued to flow through the fractured lava toward the Snake. Today this immense aquifer extends from Wyoming to the Hagerman Valley where springs burst forth from the canyon wall at a constant temperature of fifty-eight degrees—perfect for trout farms and fly-fishermen. Eighty-five percent of the nation's commercial rainbow trout come from this valley.

A favorite Indian wintering area in an earlier time, the Hagerman Valley has mild, nearly snowless winters. Legends tell of a Snake River flowing so thick with spawning salmon that you could walk across it in some places. Now there are three dams within fifteen miles of the "Wright Rapids," and the salmon have been completely eradicated.

**192**

The window grid was carefully planned to follow the plane of the prow roofline (BELOW TOP). Wright specified in his plans that the rockwork be patterned after Fallingwater, his famous Pennsylvania house.

An ugly flagstone patio was ripped out to accommodate this smoother concrete slab, gridded to match the interior floors (BOTTOM). Wright liked to blur the notion of interior and exterior spaces, in order that the two flow together in a seamless whole.

The knee brace that forms the roof support can be seen through the tall doors leading out to a small prow deck (RIGHT). This carefully designed detail saved the cantilevered roof from collapsing.

**T**he Taliesin West chairs (in front of the fireplace) were reconstructed from a design found in the house and then upholstered in a soft mauve Ultrasuede. The small tables are original. The generous proportions of the hearth were rediscovered when a nonstructural bracing pole was pulled from the center of the massive fireplace.

**T**he dining table and chairs are original to the house (MIDDLE LEFT). All needed restoration as a result of water damage and years of neglect.

**T**he china pattern (LEFT) was designed by Wright for the Imperial Hotel of Tokyo. Today it is produced by Noritake as part of the Oak Park Collection.

Henry Whiting and Lynette Kessler, owners of this Wright legacy, are fighting for the remaining white water section of the river to be designated a Wild and Scenic Recreational River. They are outdoor enthusiasts who carry a reverence for the topography that extends far beyond their interest in water sports. Whiting spent over two years reclaiming this dramatically sited house from years of neglect and disrepair.

Whiting, whose mother's brother, Alden Dow, was a nationally known architect and student of Wright, had developed a love of architecture under the tutelage and nurturing of his favorite uncle. Schooled in landscape architecture, Whiting came to Idaho to work on the design and construction of his parents' home in Sun Valley. Soon after his arrival he set about to make a pilgrimage to the only Wright-designed house in the state of Idaho: the Teater Studio. Archie Teater, an artist, spent most of his time in Jackson, Wyoming, where he sold his oil landscapes. He and wife Patricia found this promontory in Teater's native Hagerman Valley and in 1952 persuaded a very busy Wright (intensely involved in the plan for the Guggenheim Museum) to design a studio for them. While Wright never set foot on the Teaters'

property, he requested complete site documentation, and after the completion of drawings, apprentices from his Taliesin Studio came to supervise construction of what was to be known as Teater's Knoll.

When Henry Whiting finally viewed the famous knoll in 1977, he discovered an eight-foot barbed wire and chain link fence obscuring any meaningful view of the seemingly abandoned house. Five years passed before Whiting obtained entry to the hulking shell of Teater's Knoll. There he found promise in the sweeping ceiling he had seen from the road, but the roof bracing had deteriorated, the wood was discolored and damp, and nearly all the glazing needed to be replaced. Although Whiting had not really intended to buy the property, the romanticism of the project coupled with his love of Wright seduced him into embarking on a restoration project that would span two and a half years and deliver a hands-on Wright education no formal schooling could ever provide.

Whiting was particularly dazzled by the cliff setting hundreds of feet above the Snake. Although he acknowledges that southern Idaho has no truly indigenous architecture, this

An Archie Teater original oil painting of the house is flanked by a Wright designed lamp. The owner commissioned the lamp after seeing drawings of the design.

house seems very rooted to its site. Horizontally striated rock from a nearby quarry is battered back into the hillside, while the prowlike roof is poised for flight. "The dynamic tension is what makes the house so exciting," observes Whiting. "The roof looks like it's about ready to soar away and the rock makes it settle right there."

Wright's plan called for a governing theme: a parallelogram module that dictates the angles of the walls and windows, all at either 60 or 120 degrees. The concrete slab floor is gridded with parallelograms, and walls meet at 120-degree angles instead of the more common 90 degrees. Posts between windows turn at 120 degrees from the glass, and ceiling boards intersect the rafters in similar fashion. The windows parallel the ceiling angle instead of the floor, making all the windowsills slant in concert with the roof plane.

Whiting contacted Taliesin, Frank Lloyd Wright's continu-

ing atelier/school, and found that Tom Casey, one of the young Wright apprentices who worked on the Teater Studio in the fifties, and now a senior member of Taliesin, was eager to assist with the restoration plans. Casey, who had not seen the studio in thirty years, arrived and soon made up a list of fifteen items that had to be done, from basic structural shoring to purely aesthetic detailing. Whiting's budget did not allow for all the proposals to be implemented, but he did authorize Taliesin to proceed with designs for a knee brace to hold up an ominously sagging roof, andirons for the massive central fireplace, a standing lamp, and a new patio to replace the unappealing flagstone entry. Whiting and Casey's new entry called for a scored concrete slab that would extend the feeling of the interior floor grid. Wright liked to blur the notion of inside and outside, a popular concept in much Northwest design.

▲ ▲ ▲ ▲ ▲ ▲ ▲ ▲ ▲ ▲ ▲ ▲ ▲

**F**olding doors
separate the tiny
bedroom from the
studio, and a
plywood veneered
bookcase forms the
partition wall.

Although Taliesin offered to help with the redesign of the kitchen and bath, Whiting felt that because he had lived in the house for three months before commencing restoration, he was better able to understand the requirements of these spaces, and could design them himself. Wright's kitchens and baths were never the high points of his design. They tended to be small, utilitarian, and generally windowless spaces. The Teater Studio was no exception. Both bath and kitchen and an adjoining workroom were little interior squares imposed upon the carefully composed hexagonal geometry of Wright's plan. Whiting's new design acknowledges the controlling theme of the original grid pattern and blends quite harmoniously.

The redesigned kitchen and bath conform to the 60/120-degree-angle composition, as do the built-in counters, cupboards, and bathtub. Crowning the adjoining spaces is a hexagonal skylight and interior clerestories that illuminate the newly structured rooms. Whiting's kitchen is spacious and practical, utilizing the old workroom and kitchen square footage. A stepped maple countertop provides both eating and food preparation areas, and Whiting, inspired by the existing Wright furniture in the house, designed four barstools for the counter.

The bathroom is totally adapted to the eighties, with separate shower stall and a deep tub faced in granite. Whiting admits that his bath and kitchen are the most controversial parts of the restoration, but feels that life-styles have changed dramatically since the fifties. Baths and kitchens are utilized far more in the eighties than they ever were in Wright's era. "The morning we started restoration," Whiting recalls, "Tom Casey sat down with Jack McNamara [his contractor] and me and gave us a lecture on Frank Lloyd Wright

The redesign of the bathroom (RIGHT) allows for generous lighting from the hexagonal skylight and for a granite faced tub that follows the 60/120 degree angles of the original construction.

As part of the kitchen renovation, the owner designed these bar stools for the elevated counter (MIDDLE RIGHT). They are patterned after a classic Wright chair design.

and surprised both of us by saying that Mr. Wright would view his architecture as something meant to evolve. With a new owner there would be new needs."

Whiting believes that strict preservationists miss the point about Wright's organic architecture. "'Organic' implies 'living,'" says Whiting, "which means change . . . the minute architecture becomes static, it's dead . . . perhaps appropriate for a public building, but not a home."

Teater's Knoll is still being used as an artist's studio. Whiting has placed a dance floor on the concrete grid for his wife Lynette Kessler, who is a modern dancer and choreographer. She uses the house as a creative retreat for her work in dance video.

Whiting uses the old bunkhouse, secreted into the cliff below, as his creative hideaway. The bunkhouse, or Cadenza, used by the Taliesin apprentices who lived on the job site, had actually decayed beyond salvaging, and was totally rebuilt as part of the restoration program. An impressive stone wall leads from the patio of the main house to the

Cadenza. Kent Hale, the stonemason who had originally worked on the Teater Studio, still lived in nearby Oakley where the flagstone is quarried. Whiting contacted Hale and persuaded him to work on the property's restoration. Hale, whose dealings with the Teaters were not completely pleasant, was rather reluctant at first, but he ultimately gave so much of his spirit to the restoration that Whiting marked Hale's stone wall with a plaque that commemorated the stonemason's work.

Whiting found four boxes of Teater memorabilia when he took possession of the studio. By sifting through the letters, pictures, and other documents, he was not only able to become intimately acquainted with the house, but he learned much about the Teaters. It is clear from all accounts that Patricia Teater was not an easy woman to deal with. However, her dogged persistence led Frank Lloyd Wright to design a house for Idaho, and ultimately gave Henry Whiting the chance to save a Wright house. For this lover of architecture, it was the opportunity of a lifetime!

**T**he owner's redesign of the kitchen lightened and modernized the formerly dark and cramped space. The angles now acknowledge the parallelogram grid of the overall structure.

# Mountain Magic

## SOLAR

## TECHNOLOGY IN

## SUN VALLEY

Architect Arne Bystrom carefully sited the house to blend with the terrain. Long embracing walls project from the sides, holding terraces and rockery. Landscape architect Robert Murase selected minimal upkeep plantings to enhance the natural beauty of the site. The roof suggests gull wings, gently spreading out and sheltering the massive structure.

Architect Bystrom said, "The real test of an architect is stairway design." This cylindrical masterpiece (LEFT) is composed of fir and redwood, with treads of cherry and maple.

The land surrounding Sun Valley, Idaho, is pretty much the same as when Ernest Hemingway fell in love with it: wild, uncrowded, unmistakably Western. Stand in the valley and mountains loom in every direction: the Pioneers, Smokies, Boulders, White Clouds, and the jagged Sawtooth Mountains. The Sun Valley community speaks more eloquently of man-made glamour: luxurious ski condominiums, upscale mountain chalets, and a world-class resort. But take a step outside the narrow confines of resort development, and a stupendous display of natural wonders give ample testimony to the real reason people have continually been drawn to this remote part of the Northwest. It is an outdoorsman's paradise.

Although the valley has long been associated with skiing, the summer and fall months draw hunters, hikers, fishermen, and bicyclists. Summer ice shows at the Sun Valley Ice Skating Rink feature world-class skaters. Sixty miles to the north the picturesque western town of Stanley is home base for the outfitters of float and kayak excursions on the Salmon River and horsepacking into the Sawtooths.

Originally settled as part of the Warm Springs mining district, the town of Ketchum forms the nucleus of the valley. In 1936 Averell Harriman, chairman of the board of the Union Pacific Railroad, hired an Austrian, Count Felix Schaffgotsch, to search out a location for an American destination ski resort. The site had to satisfy four requirements: there should be dry powder snow, no harsh winter storms, the sun had to shine all day, and it should be serviced by the Union Pacific line. The count scoured the western United States and, after nearly giving up, wired Harriman to announce that he had found what would soon be called the St. Moritz of America.

A massive publicity avalanche soon buried the valley in celebrities. The Union Pacific constructed a world-class hotel and grounds. The Astors, the Mellons, the Whitneys, and the Rockefellers came. Norma Shearer, Gary Cooper, Claudette Colbert, Errol Flynn—all lent their names to promote an area that boasted the first chair lift and a romantic ruggedness, which was to linger long after similar resorts siphoned away attention.

▲ ▲ ▲ ▲ ▲ ▲ ▲ ▲ ▲ ▲ ▲

**A**n intimate seating area surrounds the fireplace, perfect for after-ski warming. The fireplace has a set of butterfly valves on the exterior wall to use outside air for the dying fire, another energy conservation device.

The owners of this high tech ski lodge were attracted to Sun Valley for the very reasons Schaffgotsch chose it. They wanted an area just remote enough to discourage rampant tourism, safe winter weather for flying their small airplane, plenty of powder skiing, and, most important, ample sunshine, so they could indulge a growing passion: to build an ultrasophisticated solar house that would not only be efficient but attractive.

"I'd gotten interested in solar energy," remarked the owner, a venture capitalist and trained engineer who had worked with many high tech companies. "I wanted to answer a question in the building of this house: If you start out with a clean piece of paper and a competent architect, is it

possible to build a highly energy-efficient house which is attractive, warm, and inviting? Or does an energy-efficient house by definition have to appear hacked up and tacked on to?" Most of the solar houses he had seen looked as if afterthoughts and compromises dictated the end result.

His clean piece of paper was a two-and-a-half-acre parcel of land next to the Trail Creek portion of the Sun Valley golf course. The architect was suggested by a friend, Ian Mackinlay, who had written a book on snow country design and who eventually became a consultant on the job.

Mackinlay referred the owners to Arne Bystrom, an award-winning Seattle architect who impressed them with his use of woods and natural materials. Bystrom recalls, "They wanted

something warm. I wanted to do something out of wood. The richness and complexity of the house just evolved. I don't think any of us counted on it being this rich.''

The house unfolds in three stages, three levels of perception. First you have the experience of seeing the house as a whole, a technological masterpiece with its massive support system and solar collectors. Then, upon entering, you are struck with the quality of detail, the incredible complexity of finish carpentry and interlocking wood. Finally you settle in and enjoy the intimacy of smaller, humanly scaled spaces.

The house was designed around two specific requirements: one was the solar proviso and the other was the dimensions of rooms and living spaces. The owners had lived

**B**ecause a solid three-quarter-inch slat of redwood cannot be bent, the rounded members of the staircase (FAR LEFT) are composed of three one-quarter inch slats of redwood steamed and laminated together.

**H**eat in the solarium (MIDDLE LEFT) is regulated in part by the blinds along the south wall, all computer controlled for maximum sun gain or shading.

**F**our guest bedroom suites open onto the solarium, each with its own bathroom and dressing area (ABOVE LEFT).

**T**he stairway to the master bedroom (ABOVE) is so meticulously joined that even the bolt holes are covered with redwood plugs. The house has more than two miles of laminated wood.

The living room is set off from the dining room and kitchen area by a small staircase. The master bedroom sits directly above.

Large scale furniture was chosen for the gathering areas (RIGHT) to provide a cozy retreat. The winter wool upholstery is slipcovered in the summer with off-white linen. San Francisco interior designers Tedrick & Bennett Associates spent three years designing the furnishings.

**J**ust steps away from the elaborately crafted interiors lies the heart of the house, the mechanical room with its computerized building-management and control systems, plus a dazzling array of tubes, pipes, heat exchangers, and hot water tanks (TOP RIGHT).

**F**ound space at the base of the central staircase, enfolded by lattice, houses a computer niche and a solitary workspace (BELOW RIGHT).

**A** guest bathroom (FAR TOP RIGHT) with incised pattern on every third redwood coursing. Counters are laminated strips of redwood and fir.

**T**he master bath (FAR BOTTOM RIGHT) is enclosed by a fir and redwood surround, a warm alternative to the original proposal of granite or aggregate. The screens at tub end are replaced in wintertime by insulated shutters.

in many houses and had thought a great deal about the size of rooms and what felt comfortable. What they did not calculate was the size of the stairwells and the solar gallery. The gallery is a sawtooth of greenhouses along the facade that forms a hallway of undulating size. No one, including the architect, ever imagined the massive scale of the roofline and overhang, but when the solar requirements were met, the project grew to accommodate them. Three thousand square feet of the total house are devoted solely to mechanics. The basic footprint of the rooms, so carefully plotted in the beginning, preserves the intimacy of living spaces.

The floor plan calls for a living area with sunken fireplace and built-in seating, an adjacent game area, a dining room and open kitchen, a master bedroom and bath, and four guest bedrooms with adjoining baths and dressing areas. A wine cellar, storage room, and elaborate mechanical room occupy the basement of this 8,600-square-foot retreat.

An honest desire to advance research in state of the art solar residences led this couple to choose quality at every turn. While Bystrom set out strategies for advancing that cause, the ENSAR Group of Lakewood, Colorado, energy conservation experts, set about to provide solar options. The house had to stretch out in order to maximize southern exposure, thus the long zigzag floor plan that opens to the greatest concentration of sun. The rear of the house is bermed into the hillside, to minimize heat loss during the winter as well as provide cooling capabilities in the summer. Cool air is actually drawn through shafts in the berm on frequent ninety-degree summer days. The roofline sheds back to keep the snow from precipitously sliding into the entryway.

ENSAR built a simple model to show the way the house would operate, tilting the model to determine various angles of the sun at different times of the year. They came up with reams of computer numbers and suggested solid walls in certain locations to reduce heat loss. Bystrom's plan had been particularly sensitive to the grandeur of the surrounding topography, and the owners were reluctant to give up their window on the world. When reduction of the glazing seemed too drastic a trade-off, ENSAR suggested heat mirror glass, two sheets of glass with a layer of low-emissivity plastic film between. To further insulate the window from heat loss, argon, an inert, low conductive gas, fills the spaces between

**E**ach bedroom suite has its own climate control. The window sash are all operable. In this guest bedroom, the cabinetry shows the same lavish sense of craftsmanship displayed throughout the house.

**209**

the glass and plastic. The plastic film is coated to form a one-way infrared mirror so that when the heat hits the mirror it bounces back into the room. This impressive assemblage boosted the insulation to an R value of 5 (as compared to 2.7 for triple glazing). Even more impressive are the north facing windows, which use the same system in triplicate: three panes of glass, two heat mirrors, and three cavities filled with argon for an R value of 6.7.

The active solar collectors, panels suspended from the roofline in almost nautical fashion, are composed of a series of evacuated tubes that transfer heat to oil-filled headers. This heat is in turn transferred through insulated pipes to hot water tanks that can heat 1,000 gallons of water each day. Computer-controlled blinds track the sun, and clerestory windows are programmed to release rising heat in the summer. In colder months the same rising heat is recirculated through the house by means of destratification tubes that pull the heat from high in the gallery to a rock bed below grade.

An elaborate control room orchestrates the technological harmony of this engineer's dream. Yet the seamless integra-tion of old-fashioned craftsmanship gives the house its real lyricism. The finely tuned detailing of fir and redwood, aggregate and tile, courses through the house, defining each surface, describing each space. Elaborate stairwells of carefully joined bands of wood, stair treads, counters, closets, ceilings, windows, and cabinets constructed of intricately inlaid red and blond strips permeate the construction. Every detail is thought out precisely and completely. Even the concrete walls, which are designed to be passive solar collectors, are banded with wood or tile at two-foot intervals in order to break up the mass of stone.

Bystrom's original concept was that the poles outside would be rough telephone poles, and the interior beams would be resawn. In the extraordinarily dry air of the valley, however, he began to worry that the massive supports would twist and shrink, changing dimension and compromising the stability of the roof. He then turned to glu-lam beams, laminated redwood columns that could be built to specification. This decision changed the whole nature of the house, especially the finish detail. With glu-lam, all surfaces are sanded

and finished, a much more polished look. Originally the concept was going to be quite rustic.

Bystrom was pleased with the glu-lam for many reasons, one was the pleasure of finding a substitute for hard-to-find old-growth timber. "We can still make things out of wood," says Bystrom. "They'll just be smaller pieces. It's something we'll have to live with as our forests are being mined."

The house has proved to be immensely satisfying, not only because of the technological achievement, but because of the seamless integration of art and artifice. The mechanical monster was buried within the warmth and detail of the structure, and it works! However, the owners are quite candid about the cost-effectiveness of their creation. If they live to be a thousand, they would not recoup their costs. But that was not the point! They have advanced the cause of solar technology by creating an efficient, aesthetically pleasing state of the art solar home that offers excellent ideas that others can use in more cost-effective ways.

Ironically, they conclude, "We set out to build a small ski cabin . . . and it kinda got out of hand."

The open kitchen (LEFT) is the natural hub of the living area. Divided into three distinct areas with ample circulation, there is space for cleanup, food preparation, and serving.

The serpentine gas cook-top (ABOVE) is oriented to the living spaces so the cook is never far from the action.

The solarium hot tub (FAR LEFT) can be programmed for temperature by telephone via the central computer.

Carefully terraced courtyards and patios course across the front of the house (LEFT), providing both privacy and respite. The patio walls, like river rock, collect the heat of the day, then radiate the warmth at night for dining under the stars.

213

# Stucco and Timber

A

SUN VALLEY HOUSE

DRAWS UPON

SOUTHWEST ARCHETYPES

The snow-covered slopes of the Pioneer Mountain Range tower over the house, which borders a 9.5-acre greenbelt in Idaho's Wood River Valley. Log walls are laid in a cruciform that extends outside, forming courtyards around the house.

A steer skull adds a Southwest touch to the front door (LEFT). The adjacent windows minimize the visual break between the interior and exterior log wall.

When Averell Harriman developed America's first luxury ski resort in the midst of the Great Depression, he couldn't have chosen a more appropriate name than Sun Valley. Cradled in the foothills of the Pioneer Mountain range, the Idaho town boasts an average of 310 cloudless days a year. Its slopes, scenery, and cosmopolitan atmosphere attract over 100,000 vacationers annually.

Like the Wood River Valley's 5,000 other full-time residents, Barbi Reed and Bill McDorman are able to enjoy year-round what others can only savor a week at a time. The house they have built takes advantage of the region's amenities, marrying sophisticated styling with environmental sensitivity, as befits the owners of an art gallery and a seed company.

The couple challenged designer Jim Ruscitto of Ruscitto/Latham/Blanton, Architects, to create a log house that was both contemporary and energy-efficient—a tall order, since logs are by nature an inflexible building material prone to gapping and air infiltration as they settle.

Ruscitto overcame these obstacles by placing log partitions inside a conventional frame shell. The resulting home celebrates the beauty of the logs without subordinating itself to the material's limitations. The log walls are laid out in a cruciform that divides the interior space and extends out into the surrounding yard, providing a transition between the interior and the exterior, the natural and the man-made. The courtyards created by these "flying buttresses" give the owners added privacy and instill a sense of intimacy within the vastness of the surrounding landscape.

By contrast, the outside of the home is spare and refined, its boxy, stucco-covered form recalling the adobe houses of the American Southwest. The flush windows and flat roof provide a cool, contemporary contrast to the random ruggedness of the logs. Gently rounded corners soften the angularity of the taupe exterior, which the owners matched to the color of the soil on the neighboring hills.

Over 6,000 lineal feet of hand-peeled lodgepole pine went into the construction of the house. McDorman, who acted as his own contractor and did much of the labor, used an ancient Swedish coping method to hand-scribe each log to fit snugly against the log beneath it, alleviating the need for

The house was built on pilings so as not to intrude on its natural setting, which includes dense groves of willows and a small stream.

217

**L**og walls protrude from the stucco shell of the house, tempering the severity of the Southwest styling while uniting the house with its rustic setting.

chinking between rows. The walls' ragged, unaligned ends, though painstakingly arranged, suggest the natural randomness of trees growing in the woods.

Construction lasted fifteen months—enough time to re-evaluate every detail along the way. Windows were relocated to take maximum advantage of the views. The couple is still surprised by the vistas that emerged, like the view of Mount Baldy framed by the tall, narrow window adjoining the staircase; the panoramic view of the surrounding mountain peaks offered by the ceiling-hugging clerestories; and the elk-dotted hillside that greets the owners every morning from the window outside their bedroom.

Floors throughout the main level are covered in five and a half tons of Three River Rock, a sedimentary stone native to the region. Ripples in the surface of the stone indicate the presence of an ocean over that part of Idaho at one time. The rock sits on a bed of concrete embedded with nearly a mile of rubber tubing. Hot water passing through the tubes heats the stone and, in turn, the interior.

Although electric rates are fairly low in Idaho, owing to the abundance of hydroelectric power, the owners were eager to harness the sun's rays as much as possible. They spent several years charting the course of the sun over the property before commencing construction. Oversized windows on the south side admit the low winter sun, which strikes the rock floors, heating them and the three inches of concrete they rest upon. The floor's mass retains the heat, releasing it gradually after the sun has set. In winter, when the mercury dips below zero, the backup heat doesn't kick on until after midnight. Even in subzero weather, the house remains warm well into the evening.

In summer, the home's orientation and protruding log walls shield the floor from the sun's warming rays. What heat *is* absorbed quickly dissipates into the cool mass. Despite outside temperature fluctuations of as much as forty degrees in a single day, the home maintains a consistent temperature year-round due to the extensive insulation and the thermal mass of the log walls and floor.

The 3,500-square-foot house is situated at the entrance to what was once a flourishing gold and silver mine. Unable to skirt the stream running through the middle of the property, Ruscitto decided to incorporate it into the house's design.

**T**he sinuous curves of the living room staircase and balcony (ABOVE) offset the house's austere lines. The radiant-heated floors are covered in native stone. The stripped mountain-maple chair is by Don King, the ladder is by Daniel Mack, and the painting on the far wall is the work of Montana artist Theodore Waddell.

**A** small stream runs beneath the bridge connecting the main part of the house to the master bedroom suite (FAR LEFT). The owners say they pause and listen to the gurgling of the water when they walk through the passage.

**A** quartet of tree trunks, ranging in age from 250 to 400 years old, frame the front entry (MIDDLE LEFT). The trunk at right was cut too long. Instead of lopping off the excess, the top was sculpted into a seat for the balcony above.

The water wends its way through a courtyard, passing beneath an enclosed glass bridge linking the main part of the house to the pavilion like master suite. The stream was widened in two places, forming small ponds, the larger of which is home to a half-dozen mallards in summer. The owners claim the trickling water has had a calming effect on them, inspiring them to pause and listen every time they pass from one part of the house to the next.

Flowing underground water on the site prompted Reed and McDorman to build the house on pilings—seventy-two in all. The move was intended to preserve the natural setting as much as possible and permit construction closer to the willows that flourish on the site. Three varieties—red, yellow, and silver—surround the house in lush foliage from May to November. The pie-shaped lot culminates in a meadow of Kentucky bluegrass, naturalized to the region since its introduction around the turn of the century.

The large-scale interior of the house takes its cue from the dramatic scenery and from the commanding presence of the logs. The front door opens onto a two-story entry framed by a quartet of Douglas fir columns. The columns range in age from 250 to 400 years old, with the largest measuring thirty-seven inches in diameter. All were dead when cut for the house.

One of the columns is taller than the others. Rather than lopping off the extra height, the top was sculpted into a seat that pokes up through the floor of the loft walk above. The loft overlooks the two-story living room and family room; its sinuous twists and turns providing a curvaceous counterpoint to the linearity of the log walls. A sweeping radial staircase, engineered and built by furniture-maker and designer John Erickson, connects the loft with the main floor below. The staircase had to be built freestanding, so as not to come in contact with the log walls, which settle as they dry.

Leather-backed Equipales chairs, Native American rugs, contemporary folk art, and a peeled mountain maple chair add to the house's Southwest ambience. The sculpted fireplaces and soaring chimneys are contemporary reinterpretations of traditional Southwest forms.

The greenhouse windows flanking the family room enclose a planting trough that extends down into the soil beneath the house. The hot water tubing that runs beneath the floors

**T**he staircase had to be built freestanding, since log walls settle as they dry.

**M**exican chairs and colorful contemporary folk art add to the Southwest ambience in the family room (LEFT). The adjacent kitchen features extra-deep maple counters inset with a planter for growing fresh herbs and edible flowers.

warms the soil in this trough, as well, permitting the owners to grow vegetables indoors all year long. "We find ourselves gardening almost every day," says McDorman, whose seed company specializes in high-altitude varieties of wildflowers, vegetables, and native grasses. "It's such a wonderfully peaceful activity to garden here in the middle of winter."

A copper planter is inset into the kitchen counter behind the sink. Herbs and edible flowers flourish within easy reach of the cook, and can be watered using the sink sprayer. Grow lights overhead supplement the short winter days.

The countertops are extra-deep to accommodate the planter and appliances and still leave plenty of room for cooking. Work surfaces are maple, as is the floor, which has been built like an aerobics floor to feel more comfortable underfoot. A walk-in pantry is sandwiched between the kitchen and the north-facing garage, keeping foods cool naturally.

Bathroom countertops throughout the house are covered in Three River Rock, and the master bath features a corner spa encased in the stone. The tub overlooks a grove of willows and the nine-and-a-half-acre greenbelt beyond.

The logs walls are such a formidable presence that the house doesn't cry out for much furniture. ''We found that the less we put in here, the more comfortable it seemed,'' says Reed. One piece that more than carries its weight, however, is the handsome four-poster bed that artist Ron Smith fashioned for the master bedroom from peeled lodgepole pine. Reed designed the piece, which she modeled after old New England four-posters. While its materials and form evoke the past, the bed is very much of the present—just like the house it sits in.

**T**he raised hearth (ABOVE) allows the owners to enjoy a fire while lying in bed. Craftsman Ron Smith fashioned the four-poster from peeled lodgepole pine.

**T**he dressing room vanity (FAR LEFT) is topped with Three River Rock and fitted with door handles fashioned from peeled mountain maple by craftsman Don King.

**P**erfect for ski-weary muscles, the spa (MIDDLE LEFT) overlooks a grove of willows and is encased in a surround covered with Three River Rock.

One of the entry columns pierces the balcony above, forming a seat. The clerestory windows skirting the living room make the ceiling appear to float, while framing views of the surrounding mountain ridges.

A pair of Equipales chairs, an antique wicker rocker, and an old Navajo blanket transform a corner of the balcony into a cozy sitting area (RIGHT). The ends of the log walls were kept ragged to preserve a sense of the wood's untamed naturalness.

# SOURCES

The following list of stores, services, and publications was compiled by the authors with help from the homeowners and designers represented in this book. While by no means comprehensive, we believe it represents some of the finest businesses catering to the home design field in the Northwest.

## ANTIQUES & ACCESSORIES

ABACUS ANTIQUES
204 NW Twenty-third Avenue
Portland, OR 97210
(503) 222–4688
**Korean, Japanese, and Chinese furniture, porcelain, and folk art.**

BOB ALSIN ANTIQUES
1114 Post Avenue
Seattle, WA 98101
(206) 624–9799
**English and French country pine and period oak and walnut furniture.**

THE ANTIQUES GALLERY
123 South Jackson Street
Seattle, WA 98104
(206) 340–0444
**Decorative arts and furniture from the seventeenth, eighteenth, and nineteenth century.**

BOGART BREMMER & BRADLEY ANTIQUES
8000 Fifteenth Avenue Northwest
Seattle, WA 98117
(206) 783–7333
**Turn-of-the-century American oak furniture; restored antique plumbing and lighting.**

CRAFTSMAN ANTIQUES, INC.
1520 East Olive Way
Seattle, WA 98122
(206) 324–4961
**American Arts and Crafts furniture and accessories.**

JANET DUNBAR INTERIORS
Walnut Avenue Mall
Ketchum, ID 83340
Mailing address:
P.O. Box 204
Sun Valley, ID 83353
(208) 726–8573
**Showroom of English antiques, hand-painted furniture, decorative kitchen items, upholstered pieces, and accessories. A.S.I.D. certified interior design service available.**

FT. DALLES ANTIQUES
1314 East Tenth Street
The Dalles, OR 97058
(503) 296–5122
**American primitive decorative art and collectibles.**

GAINES/HALLIDAY, INC.
1121 First Avenue
Seattle, WA 98101
(206) 464–0807
**Eighteenth- and nineteenth-century European and American antiques and art objects.**

JANE GATES ANTIQUES
622 SW Twelfth Avenue
Portland, OR 97205
(503) 228–3656
**European and American antiques.**

HAGEMAN ANTIQUES
119 South Jackson Street
Seattle, WA 98104
(206) 467–1535
**Paintings, furniture, and general antiques from the eighteenth, nineteenth, and twentieth centuries.**

HONEYCHURCH ANTIQUES
1008 James Street
Seattle, WA 98104
(206) 622–1225
**Fine Asian art and antiques from the Chinese Neolithic period (3,000 B.C.) up to the late nineteenth and early twentieth centuries.**

JAPANESE ANTIQUITIES GALLERY
200 Boston Street
Seattle, WA 98102
(206) 324–3322
**Japanese folk arts from before 1900.**

JO-JE LIMITED
2430 SW Vista Avenue
Portland, OR 97201
(503) 223–8094
**European antiques and Chinese porcelain.**

KAGEDO
55 Spring Street
Seattle, WA 98104
(206) 467–9077
**Japanese folk art and antiques, with an emphasis on ceramics, furniture, and paintings.**

KAGEDO II
1100 Western Avenue
Seattle, WA 98104
(206) 467–5847
**Vintage and antique Japanese textiles and decorative accessories.**

JERRY LAMB INTERIORS
1323 NW Twenty-third Avenue
Portland, OR 97210
(503) 227–6077
**Eighteenth- and nineteenth-century furniture and silver; Oriental porcelains, screens, and accessories.**

LINENS WEST
Trail Creek Village
Ketchum, ID 83340
Mailing address:
P.O. Box 2430
Sun Valley, ID 83353
(208) 726–3930
**Luxurious linens, European squares, sheets, duvet covers, and boudoir pillows. Will customize and coordinate linens for specific room decor.**

MARVEL ON MADISON ASIAN
ANTIQUITIES
69 Madison Street
Seattle, WA 98104
(206) 624–4225
**Japanese antiques and folk art, primarily from the nineteenth century. Also custom-designed jewelry and textiles.**

MICHEL'S ANTIQUITIES
Trail Creek Village
Ketchum, ID 83340
Mailing address:
P.O. Box 1597
Sun Valley, ID 83353
(208) 726–8382
**French and English antiques, pewter, decorative items, and accessories.**

PANDE CAMERON AND
COMPANY OF SEATTLE, INC.
815 Pine Street
Seattle, WA 98101
(206) 624–6263
and
210 105th Avenue Northeast
Bellevue, WA 98004
(206) 454–6263
**Dealers in high-quality, hand-knotted oriental rugs.**

SHOGUN'S GALLERY
206 NW Twenty-third Street
Portland, OR 97210
(503) 224–0328
**Specialists in Japanese tansu chests, woodblock prints, bronzewares, imari, and textiles from the Edo and Meiji periods.**

CAROL STEVENS INTERIORS
518 Leadville Avenue North
Ketchum, ID 83340
(208) 726–5100
**Furnishings, accessories, and interior design.**

DAVID WEATHERFORD
ANTIQUES AND INTERIORS
133 Fourteenth Avenue East
Seattle, WA 98102
(206) 329–6533
**Fine quality English and Continental furniture, and Japanese and Chinese porcelain and screens.**

JEAN WILLIAMS ANTIQUES
115 South Jackson Street
Seattle, WA 98104
(206) 622–1110
**English, French, and American period furniture and decorative arts.**

ART & CRAFT
GALLERIES

ANNE REED GALLERY
620 Sun Valley Road
Post Office Box 597
Ketchum, ID 83340
**Contemporary paintings and sculpture, functional art furniture, contemporary rustic furniture, and selected fine crafts.**

AUGEN GALLERY
817 SW Second Avenue
Portland, OR 97204
(503) 224–8182
**Emerging contemporary Northwest artists and contemporary master prints by New York and West Coast artists.**

CONTEMPORARY CRAFTS
GALLERY
3934 SW Corbett Avenue
Portland, OR 97201
(503) 223–2654
**Fibers, jewelry, glass, wood, and ceramics by craftspeople throughout the nation.**

LINDA FARRIS GALLERY
322 Second Avenue South
Seattle, WA 98104
(206) 623–1110
**Contemporary American
paintings, sculpture, and
drawings with an emphasis on
the Northwest.**

FOSTER/WHITE GALLERY
311-1/2 Occidental Avenue South
Seattle, WA 98104
(206) 622–2833
**Paintings, sculpture, and glass
by leading Northwest artists.**

THE FRIESEN GALLERY
391 First Avenue North
Ketchum, ID 83340
(208) 726–4174
and
Greyhawk Center
Warm Springs Village
Ketchum, ID 83340
Mailing address:
P.O. Box 1613
Sun Valley, ID 83353
(208) 726–5775
**Contemporary fine art by
nationally and internationally
acclaimed artists.**

**230**

THE JAMISON-THOMAS
GALLERY
217 SW First Avenue
Portland, OR 97204
(503) 222–0063
**Contemporary paintings and
sculptures by West Coast
artists.**

KNEELAND GALLERY
271 First Avenue North
Ketchum, ID 83340
Mailing address:
P.O. Box 2070
Sun Valley, ID 83353
(208) 726–5512
**Featuring the work of Western
contemporary artists, antique
Native American artifacts and
weavings, and contemporary
Indian jewelry.**

GREG KUCERA GALLERY
608 Second Avenue
Seattle, WA 98104
(206) 624–0770
**Paintings, sculpture, and fine
prints by contemporary
Northwest and nationally
recognized artists.**

LAWRENCE GALLERY
P.O. Box 187
Sheridan, OR 97378
(503) 843–3633
**Varied selection of art and
crafts by Northwest artists.**

THE LEGACY LTD.
1003 First Avenue
Seattle, WA 98104
(206) 624–6350
**Contemporary and antique
Northwest Coast Indian and
Eskimo art.**

MAVEETY GALLERY
842 SW First Avenue
Portland, OR 97204
(503) 224–9442
and
P.O. Box 148
Glen Eden Beach, OR 97388
(503) 764–2318
**Northwest art and crafts in a
variety of media. Portland store
features a selection of ceramics
by nationally recognized artists.**

NORTHWEST CRAFT CENTER
AND GALLERY
Seattle Center
Seattle, WA 98103
(206) 728–1555
**Sales area features pottery,
jewelry, glass, and woodwork.
Exhibits change monthly in
adjoining gallery.**

THE NORTHWEST GALLERY
OF FINE WOODWORKING
207 First Avenue South
Seattle, WA 98104
(206) 625–0542
**Cooperatively owned gallery
featuring quality contemporary
handmade furniture and
accessories.**

OREGON SCHOOL OF ARTS
AND CRAFTS
8245 SW Barnes Road
Portland, OR 97225
(503) 297–5544
**The school's Hoffman Gallery
features monthly exhibitions
and a sales gallery spotlighting
ceramics, wood, fiber work,
glass, jewelry, photography, and
prints by professional artists.**

CHRISTOPHER
PAWLIK/NATIVE DESIGN
108 South Jackson Street
Seattle, WA 98104
(206) 624–9985
**Ethnic art from Africa, Asia,
Mexico, and the Americas.**

LAURA RUSSO GALLERY
805 NW Twenty-first Avenue
Portland, OR 97209
(503) 226–2754
**Contemporary paintings and
sculpture, specializing in
Northwest artists.**

FRANCINE SEDERS GALLERY
6701 Greenwood Avenue North
Seattle, WA 98103
(206) 782-0355
**Contemporary art by local and national artists.**

SHERBURNE ANTIQUES AND FINE ART, INC.
100 East Fourth Street
Olympia, WA 98501
(206) 357-9177
**Specialists in historic Western American paintings.**

TRAVER SUTTON GALLERY
2219 Fourth Avenue
Seattle, WA 98121
(206) 448-4234
**Contemporary studio glass, paintings, and sculpture, with an emphasis on Northwest artists.**

## FINISHING TOUCHES

ANDREWS & ARNOLD
2804 East Madison
Seattle, WA 98112
(206) 328-3888 (store)
329-9117 (studio)
**Specializing in painted furniture, gifts, and antiques.**

ANN SACKS TILEWORKS
500 NW Twenty-third Avenue
Portland, OR 97210
(503) 222-7125
and
115 Stewart Street
Seattle, WA 98101
(206) 441-8917
**Distinctive handcrafted tiles, and natural marbles, granites, and slates.**

CACALLORI MARBLE COMPANY
1535 South Albro Place
Seattle, WA 98108
(206) 767-6300
**Sales and distribution of marble and granite; manufacturing of furniture pieces, fireplaces, tub surrounds, flooring, and tables.**

CITY TILE & MARBLE CO.
621 North Thirty-fifth Street
Seattle, WA 98103
(206) 633-0330
**Large selection of imported tile. Custom fabrication and installation of stone. Design consultation available.**

FINISH
520 Fourth Street
P.O. Box 2476
Ketchum, ID 83340
(208) 726-5470
**Special painted finishes for walls and furniture, including marbleizing, wall glazing, faux finishes, and custom color work. Samples of finishes and custom furniture on display.**

ANN GARDNER
4136 Meridian Avenue North
Seattle, WA 98103
(206) 547-8002
**This Seattle sculptor does cast glass tiles on commission for commercial and residential installations.**

HIPPO HARDWARE & TRADING CO.
201 SE Twelfth Avenue
Portland, OR 97214
(503) 231-1444
**Specialists in new, used, and restored lighting and plumbing fixtures and architectural hardware.**

LARRY LAUNCEFORD
9629 California Avenue SW
Seattle, WA 98136
(206) 938-1552
**Design and execution of hand-painted interior surface treatments.**

OREGON TILE AND MARBLE
2541 SE Ninth Street
Portland, OR 97202
(503) 231-0058

208 South Fir
Medford, OR 97501
(503) 776-5020

6110 Sixth Avenue South
Seattle, WA 98108
(206) 762-1858

**Importers and distributors of marble and granite (in tile and slab), as well as ceramic tile and installation products. Seattle branch is wholesale only.**

REJUVENATION HOUSE PARTS
901 North Skidmore
Portland, OR 97217
(503) 249-2038
**Architectural salvage and reproduction hardware parts. Specializing in the design and manufacture of reproduction lighting from the Victorian and Craftsman eras. Catalogue available.**

# FURNITURE

## ABODIO
1223 Western Avenue
Seattle, WA 98101
(206) 587–0516

1044 116th Avenue Northeast
Bellevue, WA 98005
(206) 455–3649

3650 South Cedar
Tacoma, WA 98409
(206) 475–7923

17636 Southcenter Parkway
Tukwila, WA 98188
(206) 575–1448

3105 Alderwood Boulevard
Lynnwood, WA 98036
(206) 774–0654

**Contemporary life-style
furnishings and housewares.**

## CURRENT
1201 Western Avenue
Suite 100
Seattle, WA 98101
(206) 622–2433
**Contemporary Italian- and
European-designed furniture
and lighting.**

## DESIGN CENTER
NORTHWEST
5701 Sixth Avenue South
Seattle, WA 98108
(206) 762–1200
**A comprehensive resource for
interior furnishings and finishes
available through interior
designers and architects, with
over 60 showrooms.
Complimentary designer
referral service available.**

## JOEL, INC.
South 165 Post
Spokane, WA 99204
(509) 624–2354
**Linens, dinnerware, gourmet
food, contemporary furniture,
and antique pine reproductions.**

## LENORA SQUARE
1000 Lenora Street
Seattle, WA 98121
(206) 621–7500
**Complete designer furnishings,
fabrics, wallcoverings, and
accessories. To the trade only.**

## WAYNE MARTIN INC.
210 NW Twenty-first Avenue
Portland, OR 97209
(503) 221–1555
**Wholesale showroom carrying
furniture, wallcoverings,
fabrics, lighting, and accessories.**

## SIMON AND TONEY
3528 NE Fiftieth
Portland, OR 97213
(503) 249–3799
**Custom-designed furniture
treated with custom-painted
finishes infusing traditional
forms and decoration with a
contemporary sensibility.**

## CHARLES STUHLBERG
FURNITURE
511 East Avenue North
Ketchum, ID 83340
Mailing address:
P.O. Box 629
Sun Valley, ID 83353
(208) 726–4568
**Full range of furniture and
accessories. Interior design
service available.**

## VOX
1109 NW Glisan Street
Portland, OR 97209
(503) 224–6821
**Contemporary European
furniture and locally designed
art furniture.**

# PLANTS

## BOVEE NURSERY
1737 SW Coronado Street
Salem, OR 97219
(503) 244–9341
**Dwarf landscaping plants and
species rhododendrons.**

## DENNIS' SEVEN DEES
NURSERY
6025 SE Powell Blvd.
Portland, OR 97266
(503) 777–1421

10455 SW Barnes Road
Portland, OR 97225
(503) 297–1058

1090 McVey Avenue
Lake Oswego, OR 97034
(503) 636–4660
**General nursery stock and
supplies; full-service florist.**

## GARLAND NURSERY
5474 NE Highway 20
Corvalis, OR 97330
(503) 753–6601
**General nursery stock. Good
selection of perennials, trees,
and shrubs.**

GOSSLER NURSERY
1200 Weaver Road
Springfield, OR 97478
(503) 746–3922
**Specializing in rare outdoor plants like magnolia and witch hazel. Open by appointment.**

HIGH ALTITUDE GARDENS
500 Bell Drive #7
Ketchum, ID 83340
1-800-874–7333
**A bioregional seed company and nursery specializing in mountain climates. Mail order catalogue available.**

LAMB NURSERIES
East 101 Sharp Avenue
Spokane, WA 99202
(509) 328–7956
**Hardy perennials and rock plants.**

MOLBAK'S GREENHOUSE
AND NURSERY
13625 NE 175th Street
Woodinville, WA 98072
(206) 483–5000
**Greenhouse, nursery, bedding plants, containers, garden accessories, and gift shop.**

PORTLAND NURSERY
5050 SE Stark Street
Portland, OR 97215
(503) 231–5050
**General nursery stock; good selection of roses and perennials.**

PRICE-RAGEN COMPANY
1000 Lenora St.
Seattle, WA 98121
(206) 292–8155
**Wholesale firm specializing in Italian terra-cotta planters, specimen live plants, garden furniture, and accessories.**

RAINTREE NURSERY
Hamlet Route 304
Seaside, OR 97138
(503) 738–6980
**General landscaping plants and Oregon native plants.**

TEUFEL NURSERY INC.
12345 NW Barnes Road
Portland, OR 97229
(503) 646–1111
**Wholesale nursery, grower, and commercial landscaper. Large horticultural supply department.**

WELLS-MEDINA NURSERY
8300 NE Twenty-fourth Street
Bellevue, WA 98004
(206) 454–1853
**General nursery stock, specializing in perennials, rhododendrons, and roses.**

WELLS NURSERY
INCORPORATED
424 East Section Street
Mount Vernon, WA 98273
(206) 336–6544
**Growers and distributors of premium-quality grafted conifers and Japanese maples, as well as a variety of other shade and flowering trees. Nationwide distribution.**

# ARCHITECTS, INTERIOR DESIGNERS, LANDSCAPE DESIGNERS

**The following designers' work appears in this book:**

## ARCHITECTS

ROB ANGLIN
Wyatt Stapper Architects
88 Spring Street
Seattle, WA 98104
(206) 587–5340

PIETRO BELLUSCHI
700 NW Rapidan Terrace
Portland, OR 97210
(503) 225–0131

THOMAS BOSWORTH, F.A.I.A.
4532 East Laurel Northeast
Seattle, WA 98105
(206) 522–5549

ARNE BYSTROM, F.A.I.A.
1617 Post Alley
Seattle, WA 98101
(206) 443–1011

JAMES CUTLER ARCHITECTS
135 Parfitt Way Southwest
Winslow, WA 98110
(206) 842–4710

LASSE K. JAAKOLA
Roth + Jaakola Architects
2405 Tenth Avenue East
Seattle, WA 98102
(206) 322–6254

GREG MAXWELL
Citigroup Architects & Planners
110 Union Street
Suite 402
Seattle, WA 98101
(206) 343–9411

JIM OLSON
Olson/Sundberg Architects
108 First Avenue South
Fourth Floor
Seattle, WA 98104
(206) 624–5670

JIM RUSCITTO
Ruscitto/Latham/Blanton,
Architects
P.O. Box 419
Sun Valley, ID 83353
(208) 726–5608

**234**

STUART SILK ARCHITECTS
1932 First Avenue
Seattle, WA 98101
(206) 728–9500

GEORGE SUYAMA
121 East Boston Street
Seattle, WA 98102
(206) 324–9060

FRANK LLOYD WRIGHT
FOUNDATION
Taliesin West
Scottsdale, AZ 85261
(602) 860–2700

## INTERIOR DESIGNERS

LEO ADAMS
3205 South Sixty-second Street
Yakima, WA 98903
(509) 966–5900

MIRZA DICKEL, A.S.I.D.
Dickel and Kramer
2892 NW Upshur
Portland, OR 97210
(503) 221–1017

ANNE FISHER ASSOCIATES
303 East Pine Street
Seattle, WA 98122
(206) 382–1400

TERRY HUNZIKER
97 South Jackson Street
Seattle, WA 98104
(206) 467–1144

JEAN JONGEWARD
INTERIORS
119 Tower Place
Seattle, WA 98109
(206) 284–1999

MICHAEL TEDRICK and
THOMAS BENNETT
Tedrick and Bennett Associates
2140 Hyde Street
San Francisco, CA 94109
(415) 771–3404

## LANDSCAPE ARCHITECTS / DESIGNERS

THOMAS L. BERGER
ASSOCIATES, P.S.
2021 Minor Avenue East
Seattle, WA 98102
(206) 325–6877

BECCA HANSON
The Portico Group
106 Lenora Street
Seattle, WA 98121
(206) 448–6506

WALLACE HUNTINGTON
Huntington and Kiest
2892 NW Upshur
Portland, OR 97210
(503) 222–3383

ROBERT K. MURASE
Murase Associates
1300 Northrup Northwest
Portland, OR 97209
(503 242–1477

RALPH WELLS LANDSCAPING
and R&R NURSERY
2004 132nd Avenue Southeast
Bellevue, WA 98005
(206) 641–5460

# PUBLICATIONS

**ARCADE**
2318 Second Avenue
P.O. Box 54
Seattle, WA 98121
**The Northwest journal for architecture and design.**

**ARCHITECTURAL DIGEST**
5900 Wilshire Boulevard
Los Angeles, CA 90036
(213) 938-3756
**The international magazine of fine interior design.**

**HG**
350 Madison Avenue
New York, NY 10017
(212) 880-8800
**International life-styles, art, architecture, and interior design.**

**HOME**
5900 Wilshire Boulevard
Los Angeles, CA 90036
(213) 938-3756
**Creative ideas for home design.**

**METROPOLITAN HOME**
750 Third Avenue
New York, NY 10017
(212) 557-6600
**Architecture, interior design, art, food, and life-styles, both national and international.**

**OH! IDAHO**
Peak Media Inc.
P.O. Box 925
Hailey, ID 83333
(208) 788-4500
**Pictoral coverage of Idaho people and places.**

**OREGON COAST MAGAZINE**
P.O. Box 18000
Florence, OR 97439
(503) 997-8401
**Bimonthly coverage of tourism, history, gardening, and food along the Oregon coast.**

**PACIFIC NORTHWEST MAGAZINE**
222 Dexter Avenue North
Seattle, WA 98109
(206) 682-2704
**Life-styles, recreation, home, and business of the Great Northwest.**

**PENINSULA MAGAZINE**
P.O. Box 2259
Sequim, WA 98382
(206) 683-5421
**Quarterly magazine covering travel and leisure on the Olympic Peninsula.**

**REGIONALE WEST**
P.O. Box 44-1463
Aurora, Colorado 80044
(303) 751-4752
**Architecture, interior design, art, artisans, and cultural heritage of the West.**

**SUNSET MAGAZINE**
80 Willow Road
Menlo Park, CA 94025
(415) 321-3600
**Western life-styles, homes, crafts, food, and gardens.**

**VALLEY**
Peak Media Inc.
P.O. Box 925
Hailey, ID 83333
(208) 778-4500
**Semiannual celebrating tourism in Sun Valley.**

**WASHINGTON MAGAZINE**
200 West Thomas
Third Floor
Seattle, WA 98119
(206) 285-9009
**Consumer-oriented publication highlighting the richness of people and places in Washington.**

235

# BIBLIOGRAPHY

## BOOKS

Bailey, Jo, and Cummings, Al. *San Juan: The Powder-Keg Island*. Friday Harbor, WA: Beach Combers, Inc., 1987

Boone, Lalia. *Idaho Place Names*. Moscow, ID: University of Idaho Press, 1988.

Berger, Brian. *Beautiful San Juan Islands and Puget Sound*. Beaverton, OR: Beautiful America Publishing Company, 1979.

Bush, Martin. *Sculptures by Duane Hanson*. Wichita, KS: Wichita State University, 1985.

Carpenter, Allan. *Idaho*. Chicago: Children's Press, 1979.

Clark, Rosalind. *Architecture, Oregon Style*. Albany, OR: City of Albany, Oregon, 1983.

Doherty, Diane Osgood. *Gearhart by the Sea*. Gearhart, OR: Gearhart Homeowners Association, 1985.

Droker, Howard. *Seattle's Unsinkable Houseboats*. Seattle, WA: Watermark Press, 1977.

Eals, Clay. *West Side Story*. Seattle, WA: Robinson Newspapers, 1987.

The Federal Writers' Project of the Works Progress Administration. *The Idaho Encyclopedia*. Caldwell, ID: Caxton Printers, Ltd., 1938.

Garreau, Joel. *The Nine Nations of North America*. Boston, MA: Houghton Mifflin Company, 1981.

Greenberg, Cara. *Mid-Century Modern: Furniture of the 1950's*. New York, NY: Harmony Books, 1984.

Hard af Segerstad, Ulf. *Carl Larsson's Home*. Reading, MA: Addison-Wesley Publishing Company, 1978.

Gulick, Bill. *Snake River Country*. Caldwell, ID: Caxton Printers, Ltd., 1978.

Kirk, Ruth. *San Juan Islands*. Portland, OR: Graphic Arts Publishing Company, 1972.

Kreisman, Lawrence. *Historic Preservation in Seattle*. Seattle, WA: Historic Seattle Preservation and Development Authority, 1985.

Lancaster, Clay. *The Japanese Influence in America*. New York, NY: Walton H. Rawls, 1963.

Lewis, Paul M. *Beautiful Idaho*. Beaverton, OR: Beautiful America Publishing Company, 1979.

Martin, Harry, and Busher, Dick. *Contemporary Homes of the Pacific Northwest*. Seattle, WA: Madrona Publishers, Inc., 1980.

Mather, Christine, and Woods, Sharon. *Santa Fe Style*. New York, NY: Rizzoli International Publications, Inc., 1986.

Oppenheimer, Doug, and Poore, Jim. *Sun Valley: A Biography*. Boise, ID: Beatty Books, 1976.

Peterson, F. Ross. *Idaho, a Bicentennial History*. New York, NY: W.W. Norton and Company, Inc., 1976.

Schmeer, Blaine A. *Pottery on the Willamette*. Canby, OR: Halcyon Publications, 1987.

Slesin, Suzanne; Cliff, Stafford; and Rozensztroch, Daniel. *Japanese Style*. New York, NY: Clarkson N. Potter, Inc., 1987.

Taylor, Dorice. *Sun Valley*. Sun Valley, ID: xLibris Sun Valley, 1980.

Uebelacker, Morris. L. *Time Ball*. Yakima, WA: The Yakima Nation, 1984.

Vaughan, Thomas, and Ferriday, Virginia Guest. *Space, Style and Structure*. Portland, OR: Oregon Historical Society, 1974.

Whiting, Henry, II. *Teater's Knoll*. Midland, MI: Northwood Institute Press, 1987.

Woodbridge, Sally B., and Montgomery, Roger. *A Guide to Architecture in Washington State*. Seattle, WA: University of Washington Press, 1980.

## PERIODICALS

Canty, Donald. "Portland." *Architecture*, July 1986, pp. 32–47.

Droker, Howard. "Battle of the Houseboats." *The Weekly*, February 23, 1977, pp. 7–9.

Gilmore, V. Elaine. "Sun Valley Supertech." *Popular Science*, August 1986, pp. 61–64.

Helmick, John. "Reading from Right to Right." *The Nation*, March 1, 1986, pp. 238–240.

Murphy, Jim. "A Marriage of Disciplines." *Progressive Architecture*, April 1987, pp. 86–95.

Schafer, Marilyn. "Greek Revival on the French Prairie." *House and Garden*, September 1986, pp. 140–149.

Scigliano, Eric. "The Houseboat Civil Wars." *The Weekly*, October 12, 1983, pp. 31–36.

Whiting, Henry, II. "Learning the Wright Lessons." *Home*, October 1987, pp. 38–45.